APPRECIATING DIVERSITY
THROUGH
CHILDREN'S LITERATURE

APPRECIATING DIVERSITY
THROUGH
CHILDREN'S LITERATURE

Teaching Activities for the Primary Grades

Meredith McGowan
Tom McGowan
Pat Wheeler

TEACHER IDEAS PRESS
A Division of
Libraries Unlimited, Inc.
Englewood, Colorado
1994

TEACHER IDEAS PRESS
A Division of Libraries Unlimited, Inc.
P.O. Box 6633
Englewood, CO 80155-6633
1-800-237-6124

Project Editor: Kevin W. Perizzolo
Copy Editor: Ramona Gault
Proofreader: Jason Cook
Typesetting and Interior Design: Judy Gay Matthews

Library of Congress Cataloging-in-Publication Data

McGowan, Meredith.
　　Appreciating diversity through children's literature : teaching activities for the primary grades / Meredith McGowan, Tom McGowan, Pat Wheeler.
　　　xvii, 135 p. 22x28 cm.
　　Includes bibliographical references (p. 123) and index.
　　ISBN 1-56308-117-2
　　　1. Literature--Study and teaching (Primary)--United States.
　　2. Citizenship--Study and teaching (Primary)--United States.
　　3. Interdisciplinary approach in education--United States.
　　4. Education, Primary--Activity programs--United States.
　　5. Multicultural education--United States. I. McGowan, Tom.
　　II. Wheeler, Patricia Rawson. III. Title.
　　LB1527.M34 1994
　　372.64--dc20
　　　　　　　　　　　　　　　　　　　　　　　　94-4543
　　　　　　　　　　　　　　　　　　　　　　　　CIP

Contents

Section 2
Diversity in Terms of Gender Roles—
Venturing Beyond Traditional Roles
27

Section 3
Diversity in Terms of Physical Ability—
Challenge or Handicap?
51

Acknowledgments

Many caring, dedicated educators, librarians, and primary students contributed time, effort, and good wishes toward the completion of this activity book. The authors must express their sincere gratitude to these individuals for their considerable support. Without their talent and inspiration, we could not have published this work.

For their gifts of creative teaching ideas and intriguing book titles, we thank Linda Clark, first-grade teacher, Meyer School, Tempe Elementary District #3, Tempe, Arizona; Rebecca Jenkins, Youth Services Librarian, Tempe Public Library; Judy Martin, Youth Services Librarian, Tempe Public Library; Dr. Susan Martin, Assistant Professor, Educational Foundations, School of Education, Indiana State University, Terre Haute, Indiana; Jean Speight, Librarian, Arapahoe County Public Library, Littleton, Colorado; Cara Waits, Youth Services Librarian, Tempe Public Library; and Sherry Warren, Supervisor of Youth Services, Tempe Public Library.

For hours spent reviewing materials to verify that activities are workable and book selections appropriate, we thank Marjorie Cook, kindergarten teacher, Meyer School, Tempe Elementary District #3; Patty Fisher, instructional assistant, College of Education Preschool, Arizona State University, Tempe; Dr. Gerald Hirohata, certified independent social worker, Center for Advanced Psychology, Scottsdale, Arizona; Dr. Sarah Hudelson, Associate Professor, Multicultural and Bilingual Education, College of Education, Arizona State University; Rebecca Jenkins; Wei-Chen Sun, graduate student, College of Education, Arizona State University; Vivian Winter Chaser, classroom teacher, Gila Crossing Day School, Laveen, Arizona; and Charlotte Woodward, Coordinator, College of Education Preschool, Arizona State University.

For their technical assistance in preparing the text and illustrations for the manuscript, we thank Consuelo Kolbeck, administrative assistant, College of Education, Arizona State University; Gayle Korte, ESL teacher, Hudson School, Tempe Elementary District #3; Timothy Moss, second-grade teacher, Ouabache School, Vigo County School Corporation, Terre Haute; Mary Sabla, student teacher, Ouabache School; Wei-Chen Sun; Karen Wells, media specialist, Ouabache School; and Vivian Winter Chaser.

And last but never least, for the work samples that add credibility to our teaching ideas, we thank Joshua Betts, age 9, Tempe; Rodrigo Cedillo, age 8, Tempe; Rachel Korte, age 9, Chandler; Maria Macia, age 8, Tempe; Graciela Macia, age 6, Tempe; Andy McGowan, age 5, Tempe; Claire McGowan, age 7, Tempe; Mitchell Schick, age 8, Tempe; and Molly Workman, age 5, Tempe.

We could never have done it without you!

Introduction

As you browse through this activity book for the first time, you might wonder what the authors intended as they crafted its contents. The title, we believe, says it all. Our book is designed to support educators, librarians, parents, and community leaders as they help primary children (kindergarten through grade three) acquire the knowledge, ability, and disposition to practice citizenship in our democratic society. We base our efforts, moreover, on the assumption that informed, productive citizens must appreciate the diversity that increasingly typifies life in the United States.

Literature-based teaching approaches, we also firmly believe, nurture appreciative citizenship more effectively and completely than other forms of instruction. Although the responsibility for civic education rests primarily with the social studies, all subject areas should be involved in this process, notably language and the other expressive arts. Hence, we have chosen children's fiction and developed teaching activities that integrate the content areas to promote civic competence.

In the following pages, we advance a rationale for literature-based citizenship teaching that encourages children's appreciation for diversity. We then outline how the book is organized and consider how it can best contribute to civic learning in the primary grades.

Why Diversity and Children's Literature?

Diversity as a Fact of American Life

We live in a diverse society, a nation increasingly typified by the "different." America's variety hardly surprises those of us who spend time in primary classrooms. Most schools and the communities around them reflect tremendous diversity, in terms of age, gender, physical ability, and ethnicity.

Scales Professional Development School serves a downtown neighborhood in fairly mainstream, middle-class Tempe, Arizona. On their way to school, children pass a residential complex for senior citizens and the local Head Start facility. Their fathers work as laborers, cooks, and house husbands. Some mothers keep the home fires burning, but others keep heavy machinery in working order and keep family businesses operating. Members of the local community include children who face visual, auditory, and physical disabilities. Scales students, at most recent count, speak 14 languages, including Marshallese, Hmong, and Swahili. The school population is roughly 30 percent Anglo, 25 percent Hispanic-American, 20 percent African-American, 15 percent Asian-American, and 10 percent Native American.

Most educators can share powerful stories demonstrating that schools reflect our nation's growing diversity. The social studies coordinator for Los Angeles County, for example, states that his constituents speak over 40 languages. A

Kansas school administrator struggles to bridge a gap between older and younger segments of his town's population. In Nebraska, a district superintendent searches for clinicians to meet children's special needs. The times in which our schools served only *My Three Sons* and the Beaver are most certainly over, if they ever really existed.

Learning to Appreciate Diversity

Unfortunately, we sometimes seem preoccupied with separating ourselves rather than finding commonality. For democratic citizenship to have meaning and substance, differences can no longer frighten or upset us. Americans must stop seeing diversity as a problem to solve or a challenge to meet. Instead, citizens young and old must appreciate diversity as an asset that defines our national identity and an opportunity for personal growth.

We have carefully chosen the term *appreciate* after consulting our tattered old dictionary (*Funk & Wagnalls*, 1983). This aging but authoritative source indicates that when people appreciate diversity, they recognize its value, importance, and magnitude. They esteem it highly and regularly express gratitude for it.

Clearly, appreciating diversity demands more than awareness or even understanding. We take an important step toward effective citizenship when we acquire information about the many groups that make up our global community. Still, gaining basic knowledge stops short of what true appreciation requires.

Young citizens should recognize qualities that distinguish people based on age, gender, physical ability, and ethnicity. However, children should also grasp the commonalities that these traits often mask. They must command the communication and social participation skills to relate productively with others. They must have the capacity to approach diversity-related issues in a reasonable and thoughtful manner. At the same time, young citizens should remain open to the intuitions that can resolve these issues. Perhaps most crucial, they must embrace citizenship dispositions and values, particularly a respect for the sanctity of human life and a belief in equal opportunity for all people.

Plato, "the old Greek guy," as an eighth-grader once described him to us, captured the behaviors and qualities that an appreciative citizen must repeatedly demonstrate. Such a citizen thinks reflectively, feels a deep sense of commitment, and then takes action in an ethically appropriate way. As democratic citizens, all Americans must journey toward appreciation, toward civic lives in which we think, feel, and then act without bias or prejudgment.

Teachers who simply transmit information to students contribute relatively little toward children becoming appreciative citizens. What you teach primary children is less crucial than how you treat them while teaching it. To encourage appreciation, children need opportunities to interact, even vicariously, with people of differing ages, capabilities, backgrounds, and situations. They need to analyze different ways of life and to tackle, even vicariously, the problems that these lifestyles might generate. Simply put, a teacher must provide children with frequent, meaningful, and relevant opportunities to practice thinking, feeling, and acting.

Ideally, classrooms should be communities in which children interact productively, in which they dialogue and engage in conversation. Citizens of a classroom community do not sit and listen to an adult talk at them. Instead, they converse with all sorts of people about the strengths, opportunities, and trials of living in a diverse society.

Hearing "The Call of Stories"

Perhaps most crucial, appreciative citizens should both hear and tell an ongoing, richly detailed stream of stories. These narratives can take oral or written form. Or, as a preschool girl told us, stories can be "in a book" or they can be "in your mouth." As long as they are quality stories featuring real people with characters from a range of cultural traditions—including the young and the old, women and men, the enabled and the physically disabled. As long as these tales illustrate the joyful moments, the ethical dilemmas, and the genuine emotions that so often accompany diversity. As long as they offer role models without condescending or stereotyping. As long as they provoke reflection and spark lively, even spirited conversation. And as long as they are stories that call to students, touching their lives directly or indirectly.

Two educators provide solid justification for managing your classroom so children can hear "the call of stories." Kieran Egan reminds us: "Telling a story is a way of establishing meaning" (1986, 37). He argues that young citizens construct meaning "affectively no less than cognitively" (29). Because stories largely involve people's feelings, they engage imaginations and beg emotional responses. Stories not only open access to information but also supply the structure, context, and personal identification that allow children to make meaning from them. Narratives capture students' attention, focus their thoughts, and allow them to relate big ideas to intimate, familiar examples. For Egan, stories have a tremendous power, the power to hook children so they can better comprehend a diverse society.

Robert Coles has coined the phrase "the call of stories" and explored its meaning fully, especially the ways in which teaching, literature, and the moral imagination intertwine. He suggests that stories do more than inform young readers; they force them to reconsider, to pause, to take their bearings. Coles insists that, through stories, children are "treated to a narration of events and introduced to individuals whose words and deeds . . . made an impression that lasts 'longer than a few hours'" (1989, 189). He speculates that the earliest stories were constructed to help people understand life; to help us comprehend the diversity and complexity unfolding before us. Coles observes that "a compelling narrative, offering a storyteller's moral imagination vigorously at work, can enable any of us to learn by example, to take to heart what is, really, a gift of grace" (191).

Where can you find such informative, ethically compelling stories to tell in your classroom? How can you share important works of moral imagination with young citizens in a diverse society? Coles's graduate students hear "the call of stories" from classic literature. Your primary students can hear it from quality picture books and storybooks, like Barbara Cooney's *Miss Rumphius*, Elizabeth Winthrop's *Lizzie and Harold*, Berniece Rabe's *The Balancing Girl*, or Elizabeth Fitzgerald Howard's *Aunt Flossie's Hats (and Crab Cakes Later)*. Such stories about people old and young, female and male, with varying abilities and differing cultural backgrounds, can encourage children to think, feel, and maybe even take civic action.

As you consult the recommended stories and lesson ideas that follow, remember our purpose in preparing this activity book. We offer this resource to assist educators, librarians, parents, and community leaders involved in the civic education of primary children. We present books and learning experiences that might call to young citizens in a powerful way, that might encourage children to appreciate the people of different ages, genders, abilities, and cultures who enrich our society. As you ready children to practice the rights and responsibilities of citizenship, hold these words from Robert Coles in your mind and heart:

> Novels and stories are renderings of life; they can not only keep us company, but admonish us, point us in new directions, or give us the courage to stay a given course. They can offer us . . . other eyes through which we might see, other ears with which we might make soundings . . . [Characters in a story] can be persons, however imaginary in nature, who give us pause and help us in the private moments when we try to find our bearings. (159-160)

How Can You Use This Activity Book?

Structure and Organization of the Book

As you dig into this resource, you will discover acknowledgments, this introduction, 13 chapters grouped into four sections, an epilogue, references, a bibliography of resources, and an index. Within each section, chapters share a common theme, each reflecting a dimension of diversity: age, gender, physical ability, or ethnicity. The book is comprised of the following sections:

Section 1: Diversity in Terms of Age—The Measure of Days

Section 2: Diversity in Terms of Gender Roles—Venturing Beyond Traditional Roles

Section 3: Diversity in Terms of Physical Ability—Challenge or Handicap?

Section 4: Diversity in Terms of Ethnicity—Many Cultures Enrich American Life

Note that we have divided the book into sections to give order and logical flow, not to restrict your teaching options. We assigned books to particular sections and chapters based on our assessment of their primary emphasis. If, in your judgment, a title reflects multiple themes or more closely fits the main idea of an alternative section or chapter, make adjustments as necessary. Similarly, please shift activities across sections or chapters or both to fit your teaching purposes more closely.

Each of the 13 chapters offers about 20 picture books and storybooks featuring a particular aspect of a section theme. For example, chapter 1 titles emphasize "Old Helping Young," an important element in our section 1 theme of "Diversity in Terms of Age." We prioritized our book selections by the degree to which they seem to reinforce the chapter focus. Within each chapter, the "Feature Title" clearly exemplifies the main idea, and "Alternate Titles" treat key concepts directly, but not quite as forcefully or thoroughly as the featured book. "Related Titles" enrich and elaborate the chapter focus. Each chapter also provides roughly a dozen teaching activities that these suggested works of children's fiction might introduce.

We chose books for their appeal to children, literary quality, potential for illustrating a diversity theme, and readability or "listenability" for younger children. Searching for appealing titles, we examined the "Children's Choices" preference poll, as compiled annually in *The Reading Teacher*, and several bibliographical features that appear regularly in *Booklist* (e.g., "Ethnic Groups in Children's Books," "Grandparents"). To ensure that our lists include acclaimed selections, we checked recent Newbery and Caldecott honor winners and recipients of the Coretta Scott King Award, as well as American Library Association (ALA) notables.

Because our book emphasizes citizenship learning, we consulted "Notable Children's Trade Books in the Field of Social Studies," published annually by the National Council for the Social Studies (NCSS). To locate titles that focused on particular dimensions of diversity, we explored Lee's *Elementary School Library Collection*, *The African-American Experience*, Miller-Lachmann's *Our Family, Our Friends, Our World*, Slapin and Seale's *Through Indian Eyes*, Schon's *A Hispanic Heritage, Series IV*, Jenkins's *Literature for Children About Asians and Asian-Americans*, Robertson's *Portraying Persons with Disabilities*, and Carlin, Laughlin, and Saniga's *Understanding Abilities, Disabilities, and Capabilities*. To verify that selections are currently available, we checked promising titles against *Books in Print*. As a final step in our quest for meaningful titles, we read each book before including it on the lists that follow.

At this point, discussion of the term *readability* seems in order. We selected books that not only explore diversity themes, illustrate citizenship learnings, and demonstrate quality writing, but also can be accessed by most primary students. In doing so, we admit that *accessed* seems a relative term. A picture book, for example, might appear straightforward and simple, with a small number of short words that any third-grader can read. More closely examined, the text reveals complex concepts and controversial topics that might give a graduate student long pause for reflection.

Although committed to finding accessible stories, we remain convinced that low readability scores do not guarantee that young children can make meaning from a book. A tally on a readability instrument, moreover, should not mandate that a book be confined to a particular grade level. We have tried to resolve the readability dilemma in several ways. First, our selections reflect varying levels of complexity. We have provided many options so that teachers, who know ability levels better than we do, can make sensible read-aloud choices and guide young readers to appropriate titles. Second, we have recommended that most activities begin with a read-and-discuss session in which children hear the story and consider its implications with teacher guidance. Third, we have identified particular titles for use with older primary students. These books seem so difficult, abstract, or controversial that younger children might not find them accessible.

Structure and Organization of Chapters

Each chapter opens with an explanation and interpretation of the main idea that recommended books and activities will reflect. The feature title follows, accompanied by bibliographic data annotated with a story summary and explanation of the book's potential for citizenship teaching. Then we list the alternate titles, again with bibliographic information, plot summaries, and descriptions of their citizenship possibilities. We conclude with the related titles, each bibliographic entry supplemented by a brief plot description.

An analysis of teaching options follows the book lists. Then we present a collection of ideas for citizenship teaching suggested by the feature, alternate, and related works. Every chapter offers about a dozen teaching ideas grouped into three categories, reflecting the three dimensions of citizenship that Martorella (1985, 12-13) characterized with the images of Head, Hand, and Heart:

Activities of the Head: Building Citizenship Understandings. Children collect information, process this knowledge, construct meaning from it, reflect on its implications, and make decisions based on it.

Activities of the Hand: Building Citizenship Skills. Children acquire or reinforce abilities needed for appreciative citizenship, such as geography, communication, and social participation skills, then apply them to solve real-life problems.

Activities of the Heart: Building Citizenship Dispositions. Children have opportunities to experience and analyze the dispositions that enable them to appreciate diversity, including empathy, self-esteem, respect for human dignity, and a belief in equal opportunity for all people.

Like the book's division into sections and chapters, activity categories are constructions that can become arbitrary at times. Several extended activities, for example, promote multiple skill areas and nurture key dispositions while introducing new information. Such activities meet a range of intents and seem to defy classification by a single purpose. We place learning experiences under particular headings not to restrict possibilities, but as an organizational device. Emphasize aspects of an activity you feel most appropriate or expand your teaching into uncharted areas, whatever our label might be.

Within each activity summary, we highlight the primary purpose or purposes in bold-face type. The titles that most closely fit the teaching idea are suggested as read-aloud books. We also outline step-by-step procedures for the activity and describe the teacher's role in detail. We specify necessary materials and identify possible resources (e.g., guest speakers, field trips, media). Typically, we sketch enrichment experiences that extend and expand the basic activity.

How Should You Use This Activity Book?

With each chapter, we examine your teaching options, offering tips and hints to maximize the effectiveness of recommended activities. In our epilogue, we respond to this question in a more general sense, exploring issues you should address and strategies you might use to promote appreciative citizenship.

Our recommended activities reflect, we hope, our conviction about teaching the Head, Hand, and Heart of citizenship in the primary grades. Young children acquire civic competence most effectively when they do what a citizen does every day—reflect, test, dialogue, pose questions, make decisions, and tackle problems. Their chances for building citizenship competencies drop considerably when they sit, listen, watch, memorize, repeat back, and accept unconditionally.

Consequently, we have prepared engaging, interactive, discovery-type activities. Such learning experiences require teacher openness and flexibility. They demand a classroom atmosphere that allows children to move, talk among themselves, voice opinions, ask questions, plan courses of action, make choices, and take a few chances.

As you use our book, we hope that you will mirror these expectations for young citizens. Move around to other classrooms, talk with colleagues, wonder about the viability of a teaching suggestion, adapt our plans as necessary, design your own strategies, and take a few chances. Be creative! Experiment with the teaching ideas we recommend! Get out and model appreciative citizenship in your classroom! If we motivate you to explore options for integrated, literature-based citizenship teaching, we will have accomplished the mission that launched this activity book.

Section 1

Diversity in Terms of Age— The Measure of Days

In our rapidly changing, complex, and interdependent world, appreciating diversity is central to the purpose for social studies—promoting civic competence. To help young children understand and value diversity, teachers and librarians can use literature to foster communication among age groups, bridging the apparent gap between young and old. We can show that the older citizen often shares his or her wisdom with those much younger (chapter 1), that the innocence and enthusiasm of the young can improve the quality of life for the old (chapter 2), and that the generations together accomplish more than they can apart (chapter 3). By considering and dialoguing about "the measure of days," children can gain many understandings, skills, values, and dispositions that contribute to civic competence.

Chapter 1

Old Helping Young—
The Storyteller's Legacy

This chapter demonstrates the theme that older citizens have collected considerable knowledge about the human condition and can share this wisdom in productive ways. The stories that they tell can improve the civic understandings, skills, and values of citizens much younger. In the feature, alternate, and related titles cited in this chapter, teachers and librarians will see this theme exemplified by many different people. Because it has stood the test of time and presents so many teaching possibilities, *Miss Rumphius* is our feature title; alternate and related titles reinforce the chapter theme and expand your teaching options.

Feature Title

Miss Rumphius by Barbara Cooney. New York: Viking, 1982. 32p. ISBN 0-670-47958-6.

As a child, Alice Rumphius takes counsel from her grandfather—enjoy the sea, visit faraway places, but be sure to leave the world a more beautiful place than you found it. Later, as Great-Aunt Alice, she charges her grand-niece and other neighborhood children with the same personal goals that made her long life so rewarding.

This book can reveal many social studies lessons for young citizens. Miss Rumphius is a strong female role model who takes her civic responsibilities seriously, insists on learning more about the diversity of her world, strives to improve the quality of life in her community, and encourages children to follow her example.

Alternate Titles

Good Morning, River! by Lisa Westberg Peters. Illus. by Deborah K. Ray. New York: Arcade, 1990. 32p. ISBN 1-559-70011-4.

Katherine and her older friend, Carl, enjoy the river in all its seasons, but she wishes that she could hear it "talk" as he does. Because Carl shares his knowledge and respect for the river with his young companion, Katherine begins to appreciate his special bond with nature.

Carl patiently communicates his knowledge about the river, enabling Katherine to understand her relationship with her environment much more clearly. His sharing reflects important social studies goals, including encouraging interaction and promoting geographic literacy.

Song and Dance Man by Karen Ackerman. Illus. by Stephen Gammell. New York: Alfred A. Knopf, 1988. 30p. ISBN 0-394-99330-6.

Much to his visiting grandchildren's delight, a grandfather entertains them with the vaudeville songs, dances, and jokes that he performed long ago. He transforms the attic into a stage, dragging costumes from his old trunk, singing "Yankee Doodle Boy," and performing magic tricks. The children almost forget that they are watching Grandpa and confess that his show is even better than television!

Through his stories, Grandpa enlivens the past for his grandchildren. Teachers and librarians can also breathe life into historical study by comparing and contrasting today with the old days and by illustrating how our evolving forms of entertainment have added diversity to our lives.

A Visit to the Country by Herschel Johnson. Illus. by Romare Bearden. New York: HarperCollins, 1989. 32p. ISBN 0-06-022854-7.

While visiting his grandparents in the country, Mike finds and cares for an abandoned baby bird. His grandmother helps him understand that his little patient, though very much loved, must eventually be returned to life in the wild.

Mike and his grandmother demonstrate important social studies skills in action—particularly problem solving and reflective thinking. Furthermore, their story's setting illustrates the mix of simple things and complex issues typical of country living.

Related Titles

Babushka's Doll by Patricia Polacco. New York: Simon & Schuster, 1990. 40p. ISBN 0-671-68343-8.

Grandma's doll gives Natasha a graphic lesson about treating others with respect and compassion.

Daniel's Duck by Clyde Robert Bulla. Illus. by Joan Sandin. New York: HarperCollins, 1979. 60p. ISBN 0-060-20909-7.

Daniel wants to hide the duck that he spent so much time carving until an older, experienced wood carver admires his work.

Go Fish by Mary Stolz. Illus. by Pat Cummings. New York: HarperCollins, 1991. 74p. ISBN 0-060-25822-5.

This six-chapter book features the two characters found in *Storm in the Night* (see page 5). In this book, Grandfather takes Thomas fishing and tells him stories from Africa.

Grandpa and Bo by Kevin Henkes. New York: Greenwillow Books, 1986. 32p. ISBN 0-688-04957-5.

While Bo spends the summer with his grandpa, he learns the names of birds, flowers, and grasses, as well as how to celebrate Christmas in the summer.

Hard to Be Six by Arnold Adoff. Illus. by Cheryl Hanna. New York: Lothrop, Lee & Shepard, 1991. 32p. ISBN 0-688-09579-8.

A young boy, anxious to grow up, learns patience from his grandmother.

How Does It Feel to Be Old? by Norma Farber. Illus. by Trina S. Hyman. New York: E. P. Dutton, 1988. 32p. ISBN 0-525-44367-3.

Through a woman's stories and reminiscences, age points out to youth the advantages and disadvantages of growing older.

Storm in the Night by Mary Stolz. Illus. by Pat Cummings. New York: HarperCollins, 1988. 30p. ISBN 0-060-25913-2.

By telling Thomas how he hid under his bed during thunderstorms, Grandfather helps his grandson recognize that fear is something everyone feels.

Teaching Options

As you consider the links among diversity, children's literature, and civic competence, remember Peter Martorella's notion that citizenship demands equal portions of the "Head, Hand, and Heart" (1985, 12-13). The "Head" involves gathering information, organizing it, understanding it, and then using it to make social decisions. The "Hand" involves acquiring and applying citizenship skills (e.g., map and globe, communication, and social participation skills). The "Heart" includes the values, attitudes, and dispositions (e.g., commitment, respect) that prompt us to take civic action.

The following activities can be introduced after reading *Miss Rumphius* or any of the alternate and related titles. Although most activities are not designed for specific titles, they may be better suited to some books than to others. These teaching ideas are clearly not set in stone, but can be modified to fit your teaching situation. Consider incorporating multiple books in a particular activity, allowing children to compare and contrast the many ways authors treat a concept or theme.

Activities of the Head: Building Citizenship Understandings

ACTIVITY 1. The **concept of travel** should interest students after reading *Miss Rumphius, Grandpa and Bo, A Visit to the Country, Hard to Be Six,* or *Good Morning, River!* The simple experience of visiting a neighbor or even getting the family ready to go shopping or to a movie should engage those who have not taken distant trips. Ask the children to think about the sorts of things that must be done to prepare for travel. Students from large families might categorize personal examples of tasks assumed by children or reserved for adults. Children who have traveled to other states or another country might bring in photos, travel brochures, or souvenirs to share with the class. An older person from another state or country or one who has traveled extensively might show slides or pictures of her or his experiences.

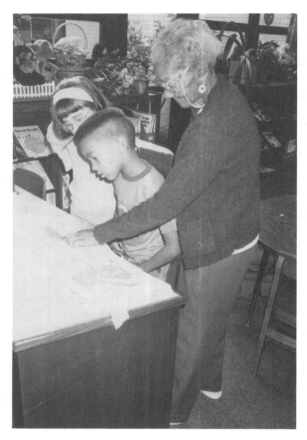

Ph.1. Senior citizen in primary classroom. *(Robert Patton, Mallory Carithers, Savanis Wilson)*

If a class seems ready to plan an imaginary trip, let them contact a travel agency, take a field trip to a local agency, or invite a travel agent to visit the class. Let the students draw on the expertise of this resource person as they plan their journey. Take cues from the students regarding the direction that their planning exercise might take and the extent to which they can pursue it.

ACTIVITY 2. Why do **flowers and other plants** play such an important part in our world? Plant life, in fact, is featured in most of the titles referenced in this chapter. To help students discover more about plants, invite a botanist from the local university, a florist, or an older person who keeps a garden to come to the school for an interview. After children listen to a storybook and consult other sources for preliminary research, have them generate a list of good questions to ask their guest.

So children can broaden, deepen, and apply their new knowledge, let them visit a library to find good books about plant life and create a classroom display. After consulting additional experts, reading related titles, and discussing what they have learned, children might take civic action by cultivating a garden and sharing produce with the needy, or by planting a tree on the school grounds.

Activities of the Hand: Building Citizenship Skills

ACTIVITY 1. Chapter 1 titles provide many opportunities for students to **apply knowledge** and **practice problem-solving skills**. After reading *Miss Rumphius* or an alternate or related title, ask children to investigate locations that desperately need beautifying. They might talk with the principal about sections of the school grounds or consult an older expert in the neighborhood for possibilities near the school. Representatives of local government might suggest locations. Once children select a target for a beautification project, have them obtain permission to plant flowers there.

Then help students list tasks that must be completed and sequence them on a timeline (e.g., choose a site, get permission, begin planning, buy seed, prepare the ground, plant seeds, tend the seedlings). Children might delegate subcommittees to tackle each assignment; they might also secure the services of an older person as project consultant. If an outdoor location cannot be found, students might plant a window garden in their classroom or build an indoor garden outside the office or in a hallway.

ACTIVITY 2. After reading *Miss Rumphius*, have students **express ideas visually** by sketching a design for a brand-new, genetically designed flower. (With alternate or related titles, children might design something else, such as a bird or a doll.) Bring in an art student or local artist, a senior citizen if possible, to help children perfect their drawing skills so they can create something truly new and beautiful. The children might try another way to express their ideas—for example, looking through flower pictures in a magazine, then making collages from cut-out parts of these photos. To conclude, have students name their creations, compare and contrast them, and ask their artist-adviser to offer his or her critiques.

ACTIVITY 3. To **build geography skills,** have students work in pairs or trios to map out trips around their neighborhood, community, or state (if children have enough map-reading expertise). Ask them to include three stop-overs, determine which routes to follow, and plot them on a road map. As they plan, students can use simple directions to state the relationship of each stop-over to the place where they live (e.g., "our first stop is due north of our town"). Each group member can investigate a stop-over site, prepare a written summary of her or his research, and include it with the group's route map. Encourage groups to seek assistance from an older person who can help them plot their trips. To conclude, provide time for each group to share its plan and let the class discuss how the trips reflect diversity of interests and backgrounds.

Consider planning other types of trips (e.g., cross-country, around the world, or to another nation). Use titles listed in this chapter to suggest other travels that children might plot on a map.

Fig. 1. An example of a flower designed by a young child. *(Claire McGowan, age 7)*

Activities of the Heart: Building Citizenship Dispositions

ACTIVITY 1. The recommended books for this chapter provide a diverse look at **how beauty touches our emotions** (e.g., rivers and thunderstorms in *Good Morning, River!* and *Storm in the Night*; pastoral settings and wildlife in *A Visit to the Country*; flowers and faraway places in *Miss Rumphius*; lovely memories in *How Does It Feel to Be Old?* and *Hard to Be Six*; wood carvings in *Daniel's Duck*; and the delight on young faces in *Song and Dance Man*).

Ask the students to **consider beauty**, then determine what kinds of things they think are beautiful and what makes them so. In small groups, let children share their thoughts. Encourage them to generate a list of characteristics that mark things as beautiful, then categorize items in a way that seems to make sense (e.g., inanimate versus living things, animal versus vegetable versus mineral).

Encourage the children to find classmates who have different views of what makes something beautiful and discuss their differences. Suggest that they include an older friend or relative in these discussions. Have children amend their characteristics after these conversations.

You might extend this activity by asking children to reread their lists, once finalized, and then create something that illustrates this view of beauty using various art supplies and media techniques.

ACTIVITY 2. As older people help the young, they **often transmit values-laden advice**. In some of the recommended titles, advice comes from the storyteller (e.g., *Storm in the Night*). It might be implied rather than stated explicitly (e.g., *Daniel's Duck*). Advice might be revealed through trickery or magic (e.g., *Babushka's Doll*).

Open a class discussion about advice. What is advice? What makes it good or bad? What types of advice do adults give children? Children to adults? Children and adults need what types of advice the most? Can you profit from advice? Must you always follow it?

After the discussion, students might write an advice column for the school newspaper or newsletter. They might interview the principal to discover what kind of advice she or he needs and then ask the student body to provide it. Have children gather advice from other school staff as well as older people in the neighborhood and incorporate these tips into the column.

To extend this activity, have students ask an older person to tell a story that summarizes the most important piece of advice they would give to a young person. Make a videotape or audiotape of the storyteller in action. Encourage students to retell the story to young persons not in their class.

ACTIVITY 3. In a large group, let children **appreciate longevity** by brainstorming all the **advantages that longevity provides**. What do students think it would be like to be old? After time to reflect, students can dialogue about this question or respond to it privately in their journals.

A read-aloud session with *How Does It Feel to Be Old?* should help prompt and guide children's reflection and discussion as the book addresses this issue directly. Other recommended titles contribute to understanding longevity; decide whether it would be better to read a book aloud to introduce the question or to culminate children's reactions to it.

To further enrich dialogue, children might ask older people what they like about being old. Classroom visitors can share what they know or can do that was beyond them when they were young. Encourage students to imagine what it will be like when they become old people and to express their thoughts in role play or artwork.

Chapter 2

Young Helping Old— The Innocent's Gift

This chapter focuses on a compelling literary theme: Though lacking experience, children can inform and inspire older people, particularly those they love. Their enthusiasm and excitement often rekindle emotional fires and replant dreams in senior citizens. In this chapter's feature, alternate, and related titles, librarians and teachers will find stories that trumpet this theme, raising the likelihood that one of their students might give a powerful, energizing gift to someone much older.

The Wednesday Surprise is our feature title because it so clearly illustrates how a young person can revitalize an older person's life and help him or her achieve a worthy goal. The alternate and related titles provide other examples of the young recharging, redirecting, and uplifting the old.

Feature Title

The Wednesday Surprise by Eve Bunting. Illus. by Donald Carrick. New York: Clarion Books, 1989. 32p. ISBN 0-899-19721-3.

While the rest of the family is busy doing other things, seven-year-old Anna and her grandmother work together every Wednesday evening. The rest of the family assumes that Grandma is teaching Anna to read; in reality, Anna is the teacher, providing skills that Grandma never acquired, despite her many years. The two reveal their secret at just the right moment—a birthday party for Anna's father.

Because it treats the importance of literacy so directly, this story is a natural for reinforcing vital citizenship skills and attitudes. Anna and Grandma believe that the written word holds great power; they also model how people can accept responsibility for teaching and learning how to read and write.

Alternate Titles

Music, Music for Everyone by Vera B. Williams. New York: Greenwillow Books, 1984. 32p. ISBN 0-688-02604-4.

Because her grandmother is sick and the family's expenses are mounting, Rosa and her friends form the Oak Street Band. The whole neighborhood enjoys the music the girls perform at an anniversary block party. All four musicians earn needed cash and Rosa begins refilling her family's big money jar.

In this book, as in *The Wednesday Surprise*, a granddaughter helps an older family member in need. She models vital social participation skills for young readers (e.g., problem solving, social interaction, and taking responsibility for one's actions). The book's setting, a multicultural urban neighborhood, might introduce additional activities in which students examine positive aspects of diversity.

When I Am Old with You by Angela Johnson. Illus. by David Soman. New York: Orchard, 1990. 32p. ISBN 0-531-08484-1.

A child imagines the things that he and his grandfather will do when they are both old together, such as playing cards, going fishing, and drinking cool water from a jug. Even now, grandson helps grandfather do these simple things and more.

The book's central characters apply basic historical skills (e.g., comparing and contrasting events past, present, and future; time-order sequencing). Also, they interact constructively, suggesting classroom opportunities for students to do likewise. Moreover, grandson and grandfather talk about wide-ranging topics and issues, modeling the reflective conversation so essential for civic competence.

Wilfrid Gordon McDonald Partridge by Mem Fox. Illus. by Julie Vivas. New York: Kane/Miller, 1985, c1984. 32p. ISBN 0-916-29104-9.

Wilfrid has a number of friends who live in a nearby home for the elderly. When he overhears his parents discussing how Miss Nancy is losing her memory, he sets out to help her. As he gathers "memories" for Miss Nancy, Wilfrid gives back her past.

In the process of helping his older friend, Wilfrid displays a number of social-studies skills (e.g., social interaction, problem solving, and information gathering) as well as crucial citizenship dispositions (e.g., empathy, respect for human dignity, the commitment to take civic action). The book also acquaints children with the inner workings of a nursing home and the ways in which many older people live today.

Related Titles

Always Gramma by Vaunda Micheaux Nelson. Illus. by Kimanne Uhler. New York: Putnam, 1988. 32p. ISBN 0-399-21542-5.

A girl is confused, upset, and sad when Gramma becomes so "mixed up" that she must have 24-hour care in a nursing home. Fortunately, granddaughter can visit frequently and cheer Gramma with familiar stories.

A Balloon for Grandad by Nigel Gray. Illus. by Jane Ray. New York: Orchard, 1988. 30p. ISBN 0-531-08355-1.

When Sam's balloon escapes out the window of his house, he is really upset; then he and his father smile at the pleasure that Grandad Abdulla will receive when the balloon sails by his home in North Africa.

The Best Present by Holly Keller. New York: Greenwillow Books, 1989. 32p. ISBN 0-688-07320-4.

When Grandma is sick in the hospital, Rosie wants to visit her but is told that she is too young. Though she cannot show her concern in person, she asks a staff member to deliver flowers to Grandma.

The Gift by Helen Coutant. Illus. by Vo-Dinh Mai. New York: Alfred A. Knopf, 1983. 45p. ISBN 0-394-95499-8.

> With her gift to Nana Marie, an older friend who is now blind, Anna promises to share the wonders of the world every day.

Grandpa's Song by Tony Johnston. Illus. by Brad Sneed. New York: Dial Press, 1991. 32p. ISBN 0-803-70802-5.

> Grandpa was always exuberant and enthusiastic. As he becomes more forgetful, his granddaughter helps him recover lost thoughts by singing their favorite songs.

How Pizza Came to Queens by Dayal Kaur Khalsa. New York: Potter, 1989. 30p. ISBN 0-517-57126-9.

> Mrs. Pellegrino seems sad during her visit from Italy and keeps repeating, "No pizza, no pizza." To solve this mystery, May and Linda visit the library, research the origins of pizza, and use their findings to cheer up their Italian visitor.

Like Jake and Me by Mavis Jukes. Illus. by Lloyd Bloom. New York: Alfred A. Knopf, 1984. 32p. ISBN 0-394-95608-7.

> Alex and Jake finally find grounds for a positive relationship when the boy helps his new stepfather confront his biggest fear—a large, hairy spider!

My Great Grandpa by Martin Waddell. Illus. by Dom Mansell. New York: Putnam, 1990. 26p. ISBN 0-399-22155-7.

> A girl enjoys special times with Great Grandpa, pushing him on walks in his wheelchair. Though his physical movement is limited, she knows that, with her assistance, he can still travel to beautiful and exciting places in his mind.

Now One Foot, Now the Other by Tomie dePaola. New York: Putnam, 1981. 32p. ISBN 0-399-20774-0.

> Bobby's grandfather helped him learn to walk and talk. After Grandfather Bob's stroke, his young grandson returns the favor.

Tucking Mommy In by Morag Jean Loh. Illus. by Donna Rawlins. New York: Orchard, 1988. 29p. ISBN 0-531-08340-3.

> In an unusual turn of events, Sue and Jenny find themselves putting their mother to bed, with all the care and tenderness that she often shows them.

Teaching Options

The following activities can be introduced after reading *The Wednesday Surprise* or any of the alternate and related titles. Although activities are typically not intended for specific titles, they may be better suited to some books than to others. Modify these teaching ideas to fit your classroom situation and the abilities and developmental levels of your students. Also consider incorporating multiple books in a particular activity, allowing children to encounter several examples of a concept or theme.

Activities of the Head: Building Citizenship Understandings

ACTIVITY 1. After reading *The Wednesday Surprise*, the class can **investigate birthdays**. Children should begin their quest for information at the public library, browsing through newspapers published during the week in which they were born. Librarians can direct children to holdings in hard copy as well as microfiche or microfilm, helping children discover and use the breadth and depth of library resources.

To focus and spark inquiry, suggest the following questions for students to answer: What were the major headlines during your birthday week? Which young people made news? Which old people made news? What was the weather like? How many babies were born that day or week? Which teams or players dominated the sports page? What interesting events occurred in your town, state, or region at that time? What was happening around the world? What did selected food items cost? What movies, TV shows, and radio shows were popular? Who had a hit record that week? Can you find photos or stories that show young and old people doing things together?

Encourage students to display their new knowledge in creative ways, such as reproducing photographs and headlines, then making a collage; singing a popular song; role-playing a memorable event. Allow children plenty of time to compare and contrast their findings.

You might extend this activity in several ways. After warming up with their own birthday weeks, students can travel farther back in time, finding birthday newspapers for an older relative or special friend. Children can then compare and contrast this information with what they learned about their own birthday weeks. Working in small groups, the class might also chart or graph the data using various categories (e.g., class birthdays by week or month, or by city, county, state, or country). Finally, students might tag their places of birth on a map, then compare these locations by factors such as weather or climate, landforms, population, resources, and major industries.

ACTIVITY 2. Even the simplest daily chores or tasks often require reading and writing. Several titles mentioned in this chapter might help children better **understand the power that words can hold**. For example, the girls in *How Pizza Came to Queens* read about pizza before they listed the ingredients that they needed to buy. Although music is not actually printed in *Grandpa's Song* or *Music, Music for Everyone*, the characters read the music at some point before playing it.

Encourage children to describe other examples of literacy in action, such as consulting the phone book before dialing a take-out restaurant, examining the day's mail, or checking the directions on a pudding box before adding milk. Introduce the term **environmental print** to label these examples. In a class discussion, examine how environmental print influences daily life, guiding children to the conclusion that literacy has great power to unlock secrets and provide direction no matter what we do.

To conclude, group students in pairs or trios and let them list all the different places or situations where they might find people using environmental print (i.e., wherever they work, shop, cook, play games or sports, find transportation, bank their money, and eat). Have each group translate a selected example into a visual display (e.g., collage, drawing, model, diorama) and share it with classmates and then another class, if possible. As the displays are presented, each group should ask audience members to describe how they might use this print item and then explain how it transforms a demanding task into a much simpler one. To conclude the presentation, help students generate and sustain a dialogue about the ways in which literacy skills influence our daily routines.

ACTIVITY 3. This activity promotes **the understanding that every family member has a role.** Though children's roles might be less obvious than adults' or parents' roles, every family member has a unique role to play. As you read this chapter's feature, alternate, or related titles, particularly *Now One Foot, Now the Other*, *Grandpa's Song*, *Tucking Mommy In*, *Always Gramma*, and *My Great Grandpa*, highlight the jobs that young family members perform. Use these examples to guide children to the realization that they make similar contributions every day. Ask students if they have daily or weekly chores. Must they set the table, make the bed, or water flowers? Are they responsible for watching a younger brother or sister or for taking the newspaper to Grandpa? Are pets dependent on them for food, water, and daily outings? Do children help get dinner ready or wash dishes? Do they call Mom at work to let her know that they arrived home safely? Does an older neighbor need help with errands now and then? Have they ever read to a grandmother or grandfather whose eyesight is failing? Students can answer these questions directly, or role-play these situations for classmates.

As an extension activity, each student could ask a grown-up with whom she or he lives to describe the child's family role, especially as it relates to older family members. Students might tape these conversations or record them in journals and share them with classmates. Then, in small groups, students might role-play chores that they perform. As a class, students might also chart or graph their family jobs by category.

Activities of the Hand: Building Citizenship Skills

ACTIVITY 1. To **build positive interaction skills** and **explore how family members can interact productively**, let students think about things they enjoy doing with a particular family member. To get students into a thinking mode, you might read aloud *When I Am Old with You*, which features a younger and an older family member working and playing together. After they have brainstormed ideas, ask each child to pick his or her favorite activity with an older family member.

Using an example from your own family life, show children that any interactive experience can be broken down into a series of steps. For example, to bake cookies with Grandma, first you get the cookbook, then you find the ingredients, then you put them into a bowl, and so on. Then demonstrate how to diagram this sequence on a **flow chart**. Tell students that a well-done flow chart allows someone else to re-create an unfamiliar experience. Have each child make a flow chart illustrating a favorite interactive experience. Pair students so they can test the effectiveness of each other's work. Encourage children to take their flow charts home and share them with an older family member or friend.

ACTIVITY 2. *Always Gramma* relates how a young girl cheers her bed-ridden grandmother by retelling favorite stories. After reading the book aloud, buddy up your students with members of another class, or, if possible, with seniors from a retirement community or a care center, to **share their reading or storytelling skills**. Once the logistics of buddying up are complete, ask each student to bring a favorite or newly discovered book or story to introduce to his or her partner.

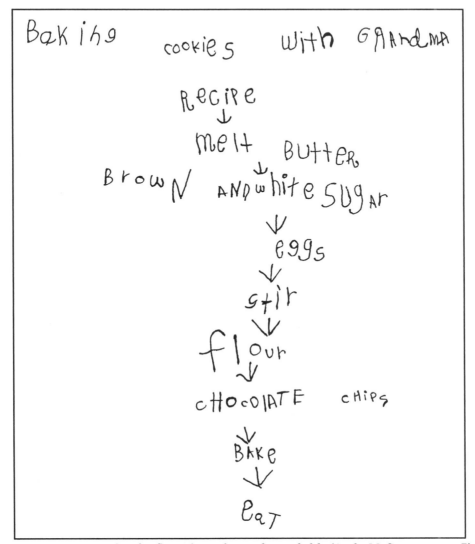

Fig. 2. An example of a flow chart drawn by a child. *(Andy McGowan, age 5)*

At first, schedule regular times for reading or storytelling, but if possible, allow sharing sessions to become more spontaneous and personal. As the sharing progresses, bring students together periodically to discuss how reading or storytelling has affected them and their partners.

ACTIVITY 3. Both *The Wednesday Surprise* and *Like Jake and Me* have surprise endings that introduce opportunities to **practice writing skills**. After reading aloud one or both of these books, talk about parts of a story with children, particularly how an author can craft a story that takes a sudden turn. Conclude with a writers' workshop in which children write stories about a current event, place, or person that twist in unexpected directions. If possible, publish these works or let students create a bulletin board to display them; at the least, provide time for children to dialogue about their writing efforts.

Activities of the Heart: Building Citizenship Dispositions

ACTIVITY 1. This activity allows students to **appreciate differences** by seeing a familiar example of diversity in action. Everyone has a birthday, but not everyone celebrates it the same way. Ask students to think about the food, games, music, decorations, places to go, and gifts that make up their celebrations. If time permits, each child might draw a "photograph" of her or his most recent party. Class members can then compare and contrast the ways in which they put on a birthday bash. During their conversations, help them realize that certain values and attitudes—love, family ties, pride in accomplishment, gratitude—underlie every celebration, no matter how different they might seem on the surface.

To extend the activity, ask children to brainstorm as many unique ways to celebrate a birthday as they can—serving exotic foods, playing wild and challenging games, singing a new arrangement of "Happy Birthday," and visiting unusual places. Let small groups develop some of these unusual ideas into **new classroom traditions** for student and teacher birthdays. To field-test the new traditions, introduce them at an "unbirthday party," inviting older friends and relatives as special guests. Form committees and delegate tasks so students can assume responsibility for planning and preparation.

ACTIVITY 2. This activity allows children to recognize that even the smallest gift can **nurture human interaction**. Birthdays and holidays often produce gifts. Let students see that gift-giving often occurs on less formal, though just as special occasions, by reading aloud one or more of the following: *A Balloon for Grandad*, *The Best Present*, *The Gift*, and *Wilfrid Gordon McDonald Partridge*. As you discuss the books, help students identify occasions throughout the year when they might make gifts for older family members or friends. Help children realize and share with classmates, if willing, the joy and satisfaction that an unexpected gift can bring both recipient and giver.

ACTIVITY 3. In this activity, youngsters reach out to oldsters and **share a special talent**. Teachers often find grandparents who come to school and teach children about something that happened back in the old days. This time, turn the tables and follow up a senior citizen's classroom visit with a Grandpersons' Day. Students serve refreshments and share their interests with invited older persons. As the party's main event, let small groups of children teach their guests how to do an art or craft activity, sing a new song, or practice a special skill.

ACTIVITY 4. After reading *Like Jake and Me* or *Now One Foot, Now the Other*, or both, have children find more books featuring **struggles that people overcome**. Read selected books to the whole group or have small groups of children read them to each other. Generate role-play situations in which children pretend to be characters overcoming obstacles, dealing with adversity, or tackling problems.

In small groups, children can discuss the **feelings** that a struggling character probably had at the beginning of the book, how these feelings shifted as the character tackled the difficulty, and how the character felt as the problem was resolved. To extend the activity, children can create an emotional timeline to visualize the progression of feelings, using bands of color on large pieces of art paper. Have them label each color with a sentence or two describing the emotion it represents. Older children might tape excerpts from popular songs, with accompanying voice-over explanations to illustrate how emotions change as a struggle is overcome.

Chapter 3

The Generations Together—
The Renewal of Youth
and the Flowering of Age

This chapter advances the message that the generations can accomplish more together than they ever can apart. Opportunities abound for confirming natural connections between children and senior citizens; all around us, great potential for productive kinship lies untapped. This chapter's literature selections feature positive, living examples of young-old relationships. In the feature title, *Grandpa's Face*, a girl and her grandfather forge a lasting bond that enriches both lives. The alternate and related titles feature characters and situations that further support the chapter's central theme.

Feature Title

Grandpa's Face by Eloise Greenfield. Illus. by Floyd Cooper. New York: Philomel, 1988. 30p. ISBN 0-399-21525-5.

Tamika and her grandfather spend lots of time together; one of their favorite things is going for a "talk-walk." One day, as Tamika watches Grandpa rehearsing his part for a play, she sees angry expressions on his face that she has never seen before. She becomes frightened, thinking that he is angry with her. By talking things out, Grandpa and Tamika understand more about acting, real emotions, and what they feel about each other.

With its focus on feelings and communication, this book is an excellent social studies resource. Librarians and teachers can help students explore such emotions as fear and anger. Children might also examine Grandpa's theater activities to contrast fantasy with reality. In addition, they might consider Grandpa and Tamika's interactions to better understand the power of verbal and nonverbal communication.

Alternate Titles

I Know a Lady by Charlotte Zolotow. Illus. by James Stevenson. New York: Greenwillow Books, 1984. 24p. ISBN 0-688-03838-7.

In this warm, sensitive story, an older woman and the neighborhood children build a relationship throughout the year. As the seasons progress, they plant a garden, rake leaves, celebrate holidays, and talk over lots of interesting things. Their time together yields personal growth for young and old.

This story provides an excellent model for gaining and sustaining compatibility across generations. Students can explore how mutual respect enables old and young to enjoy meaningful and beneficial interaction. The book's holiday scenes introduce special possibilities for caring, sharing, and tradition-building activities.

Mrs. Katz and Tush by Patricia Polacco. New York: Little Rooster, 1992. 32p. ISBN 0-553-08122-5.

A tentative friendship between Mrs. Katz and Larnel truly blooms when the African-American boy gives the lonely Jewish widow a kitten. Because the kitten has no tail, Mrs. Katz names her "Tush" and immediately treats her as one of the family. Larnel and his older friend spend hours together, exchanging joyful gifts. Mrs. Katz enlightens Larnel about parallels in Jewish and African-American heritage, while the boy shows the widow how to love and feel wanted again.

The book's setting and main characters illustrate key citizenship learnings on several levels. First, the story evolves in a transitional, diverse urban neighborhood, like many across our country. Second, Larnel and Mrs. Katz demonstrate how positive social interaction can benefit everyone involved. Third, their shared stories teach us that cultures and traditions may seem totally different but often rest on a common foundation.

Uncle Willie and the Soup Kitchen by DyAnne DiSalvo-Ryan. New York: Morrow Junior Books, 1991. 32p. ISBN 0-688-09166-0.

Uncle Willie and his nephew spend their afternoons together while Mom works. Mostly, they sit and pass the time after school. But one day, Uncle Willie invites his young charge to join him as a volunteer at a soup kitchen. The experience changes how uncle and nephew view the world.

Concern for the homeless and the hungry radiates from this picture book, which will add a strong sense of commitment and respect for human dignity to any social studies program. Uncle Willie and his nephew provide role models for helping others as well as a quick look at how citizens might alleviate a pressing social problem.

Related Titles

Aunt Flossie's Hats (and Crab Cakes Later) by Elizabeth Fitzgerald Howard. Illus. by James Ransome. New York: Clarion Books, 1991. 32p. ISBN 0-395-54682-6.

Visiting Aunt Flossie's house is a special event because she has so many stories to tell. As Sarah and Susan dig through hat boxes, they find treasures that prompt Aunt Flossie to share memories of Baltimore long ago.

Bike Trip by Betsy Maestro and Giulio Maestro. New York: HarperCollins, 1992. 32p. ISBN 0-060-22732-X.

Josh gets excited just thinking about the 16-mile, round-trip bike ride that all the members of his family will soon take together.

City Street by Douglas Florian. New York: Greenwillow Books, 1990. 32p. ISBN 0-688-09544-5.

> The book's straightforward text and simple illustrations capture the diversity of modern urban life.

The Day of the Rainbow by Ruth Craft. Illus. by Niki Daly. New York: Puffin Books, 1991. 32p. ISBN 0-140-50935-6.

> On a hot day in the city, three cranky people each lose something important. Rain and a rainbow cool and brighten the city as the strangers inadvertently help one another recover their keepsakes.

Dear Annie by Judith Caseley. New York: Greenwillow Books, 1991. 32p. ISBN 0-688-10011-2.

> From the time of Annie's birth, Grandfather writes postcards and letters to her. For Grandfather, it seems like no time at all before she can write back to him.

The Dream Stair by Betsy James. Illus. by Richard J. Watson. New York: Harper-Collins, 1990. 32p. ISBN 0-060-22788-5.

> As a little girl prepares for bed, Granny expresses her love and asks to hear about dreams in the morning, filling the girl's night with thrills and chills on a dream staircase.

Grandma's Baseball by Gavin Curtis. New York: Crown, 1990. 32p. ISBN 0-517-57390-3.

> A boy frets as his grandmother comes to live with his family after her husband's death. After a shaky start, the two soon discover similar interests that temper their differences.

Island Boy by Barbara Cooney. New York: Viking, 1988. 32p. ISBN 0-670-81749-X.

> The Tibbetts settled on a New England island years ago. In this lovely story, young readers meet four generations of the family happily growing and living together.

Just Like Max by Karen Ackerman. Illus. by George Schmidt. New York: Alfred A. Knopf, 1990. 30p. ISBN 0-394-90176-2.

> Aaron and Great-Uncle Max, a tailor, work on a special project after Uncle Max gets sick. Because Max cannot sew anymore, Aaron becomes his uncle's "hands" as they finish their task together.

The Memory Box by Mary Bahr. Illus. by David Cunningham. Morton Grove, IL: A. Whitman, 1992. 32p. ISBN 0-807-55052-3.

> Because Gramps realizes that he will become progressively sicker with Alzheimer's disease, he spends time one summer with his grandson, Zach, putting special things into a memory box.

Mr. Jordan in the Park by Laura Jane Coats. New York: Macmillan, 1989. 32p. ISBN 0-02-719053-6.

> The book reviews the happy times that Mr. Jordan spends in his favorite neighborhood park, first as a child, then as a parent, and finally as a grandfather.

On Granddaddy's Farm by Thomas B. Allen. New York: Knopf Books for Young Readers, 1989. 30p. ISBN 0-394-99613-5.

> During the 1930s, the author and his cousins gather many memories, spending summers with grandparents on a Tennessee farm.

The Patchwork Quilt by Valerie Flournoy. Illus. by Jerry Pinkney. New York: Dial Press, 1985. 32p. ISBN 0-803-70098-9.

> Tanya asks Grandma to make a quilt that tells the family's story. When Grandma gets sick, Tanya mobilizes her family to complete the heirloom and speed Grandma's recovery.

The Relatives Came by Cynthia Rylant. Illus. by Stephen Gammell. New York: Bradbury Press, 1985. 32p. ISBN 0-027-77220-9.

> One summer, the relatives travel over the mountains to pay a long visit; young and old pitch in to make the stay most enjoyable.

We Keep a Store by Anne Shelby. Illus. by John Ward. New York: Orchard, 1990. 32p. ISBN 0-531-08456-6.

> A young narrator describes how everyone from toddler to grandparent works together to run their family-owned store.

What Kind of Babysitter Is This? by Dolores Johnson. New York: Macmillan, 1991. 32p. ISBN 0-027-47846-7.

> The thought of having a baby-sitter brings tears to Kevin's eyes. When Aunt Lovey arrives to do the job, he discovers her hidden passion—baseball—and decides that some baby-sitters are just fine.

Window Wishing by Jeannette Franklin Caines. New York: HarperCollins, 1980. 18p. ISBN 0-060-20934-8.

> A slightly eccentric but tons-of-fun grandmother and her willing and able grandchildren illustrate how to enjoy a vacation.

Teaching Options

After reading *Grandpa's Face* or any of the alternate and related titles, introduce one or more of these activities. Most are not designed for specific titles, though they may work better with some books than with others. These ideas can be modified to fit your teaching and children's learning situations. As in past chapters, consider incorporating multiple books into a particular activity.

Activities of the Head: Building Citizenship Understandings

ACTIVITY 1. Emotions influence our relationships with our peers, our relatives, and our neighbors. To help children **better understand their emotions**, read *Grandpa's Face* aloud, then guide the children as they discuss the following: What are emotions? Who has emotions? How do emotions affect all our lives?

Ph.2. Teacher reading story aloud to children. *(Mary Sabla's class)*

After this opening dialogue, a school counselor might visit the classroom to help children reexamine these questions from different perspectives. If your school has no counselor, invite a qualified guest who can broaden and deepen children's conversations. Encourage children to ask questions or raise other issues related to personal feelings.

To carry the discussion further, other chapter 3 titles explore the many ways in which various emotions influence people's lives (e.g., loneliness in *Mrs. Katz and Tush*, happiness in *I Know a Lady*, frustration in *The Day of the Rainbow*, anger in *What Kind of Babysitter Is This?*). As you read selected passages from one or more of these stories, ask children to think about the language that authors use to capture even the most elusive emotions. Have children close their eyes, get a first impression of a particular character's deepest emotion, and draw a mental picture to hold this impression in their minds. Then show the book's illustrations so children can see how the illustrator portrayed that emotion. Let children compare and contrast their mental pictures in pairs or trios. If time allows, let children transfer their "pictures" to paper before discussing them with classmates.

ACTIVITY 2. After reading *Grandpa's Face*, *Mr. Jordan in the Park*, *The Relatives Came*, or all three, provide students with an opportunity to **examine cause and effect relationships**, particularly the ways in which different patterns of events can produce different outcomes. Ask children to think about the order in which story events unfolded. What event happened first? Last? What happened in between? Chart this sequence of events on the chalkboard or on a large piece of butcher paper.

Then, working in pairs or trios, children can speculate about how the story might have been different if this order had been changed. In *The Relatives Came*, for example, what would have happened if the visitors had arrived at the end of the story instead of near the beginning? As discussion proceeds, focus on the major issue or problem that the main character faced. Have children determine how changing events could alter this problem and dictate a fresh approach to its solution.

For enrichment, relate this activity to students' own lives. Each student can chart a simple sequence of events from birth to the present. Ask them how their lives might be different if these events had been changed in some way. What if they had been the youngest instead of the oldest child? What if they had grown up when their grandparents did? What if their family had never moved? What if their family had moved many times? Ask students to imagine what their lives might be like. Would they have the same friends? Eat the same foods? Wear the same clothes? Play the same games? Face the same problems? If time permits, students can write "upside-down" picture books that illustrate how their lives might have been turned topsy-turvy.

If this task seems daunting for your students, consider simplifying it to match their ability levels. For example, students might sequence the previous week or even the past day's happenings. Or they might select a specific classroom situation and chart the events that preceded it.

ACTIVITY 3. This activity reinforces students' **understanding of emotions** and also allows them to **practice nonverbal communication skills**. Let small groups of students choose chapter 3 titles in which characters display strong emotions. If abilities allow, each group can read its selection cooperatively; if not, ask an older volunteer or an upper-grade student to share the story aloud. In a follow-up discussion, children can identify the emotions expressed and consider their implications for other characters.

As time permits, children can act out these emotions in small or large group settings. Before the "big show," encourage students to practice in front of a mirror, watching their own faces as they show particular emotions. Remind them that body positions and hand gestures communicate an emotion as powerfully as facial expressions. Students might also practice with older friends or relatives watching and ask them how to improve the performances. Let group members guess the particular emotion on display. Conclude with a discussion of how emotions affect everyone, every day.

Activities of the Hand: Building Citizenship Skills

ACTIVITY 1. Many characters in the chapter 3 selections are visiting relatives or friends (e.g., *The Relatives Came, I Know a Lady, Aunt Flossie's Hats, Window Wishing,* and *On Granddaddy's Farm*). Explain to children that, when apart, these characters must use the telephone or exchange letters to keep in touch with each other. In *Dear Annie*, for example, grandfather and granddaughter started the writing habit early, relying on short letters and postcards to share feelings and ideas.

To enhance students' **written communication skills**, provide several writing options. They might choose Annie and her grandfather's informal way of communicating with notes and postcards. Or they might draft some other kind of correspondence. After reading a book aloud, let children pursue one of these options with a favorite character. For example, they might write an invitation to a relative to come back soon or to the lady next door for a tea party. Children might write and even send a thank-you note to Aunt Flossie for the crab cakes or to Gram for the "window wishing" expedition. They might put pencil to paper and ask Granddaddy what they should pack for an upcoming vacation on his farm.

To add **geography skills** to this activity, help children determine where each character lives in relation to your school's location. Using a wall map, pinpoint the destinations for all correspondence and ask students a few basic geography questions (e.g., which characters live near the ocean? near the mountains? closest? farthest away?).

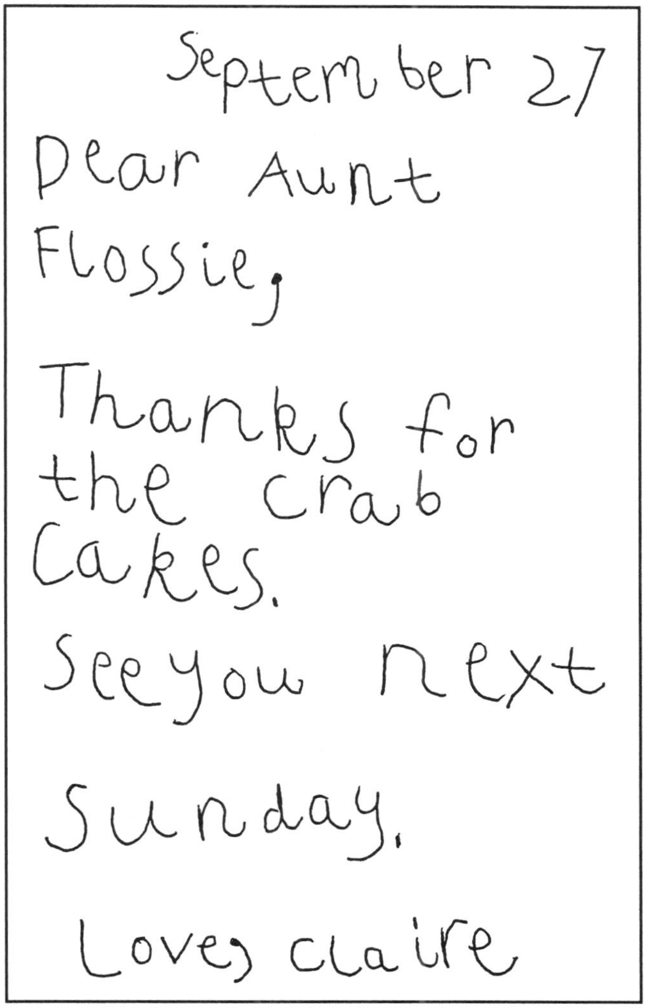
September 27

Dear Aunt Flossie,

Thanks for the crab cakes.

See you next Sunday.

Love, claire

Fig. 3. A letter to Aunt Flossie thanking her for crab cakes. *(Claire McGowan, age 7)*

ACTIVITY 2. Communication is a vital citizenship skill. Although students need to practice verbal forms of communication, they must build **skills for nonverbal communication** as well. At the very least, children should learn that people often talk without speaking and send clear messages without writing. Pantomime is an obvious example of nonverbal communication, but it can take many subtler forms. In *Bike Trip*, for example, the family bikers use nonverbal signals as they ride to and from town. As you read the story aloud, have students analyze the nature and effectiveness of these nonverbal interactions and others they might have used to communicate with each other. Then have children brainstorm ways in which they "talk without speaking" in various settings (e.g., home, school, library, movie theater, church) and discuss situations when nonverbal communication seems the most appropriate way to establish and maintain a dialogue.

To extend class discussion, arrange for students to see a play or show a videotape in which actors use hand gestures, facial expressions, and body positions to communicate with the audience. If possible, invite a senior citizen with acting experience, perhaps an actress from the local community theater or a retired drama coach, to show the class how he or she practices nonverbal communication skills. Extend the activity by having small groups write short plays (or find suitable examples from source materials) that allow them to apply what they have learned about nonverbal communication. Provide class time for the young actors to demonstrate their nonverbal skills to classmates or other audiences or both.

ACTIVITY 3. To boost students' ability to **communicate ideas through visuals**, ask children to examine an advertisement from a magazine or watch a commercial on television targeted at older citizens. Help them identify emotions evoked by the ad and discuss the reasons students think the ad was created. Then have them look at an ad or commercial aimed at children to discover whether the same or different emotions are conveyed by the style of the ad. Lead children in a discussion about how ads are designed to manipulate people's feelings about an issue or buying habits toward a product.

To extend this activity, you could invite a local newspaper or television spokesperson to visit and talk about advertising strategies that work best with different age groups. Conclude the activity by having students create advertisements or commercials designed to evoke a particular emotion in a targeted age group.

ACTIVITY 4. This activity demonstrates how **storytelling skills** can sway listeners of all ages. Following a read-aloud session with *The Patchwork Quilt, Aunt Flossie's Hats, Mrs. Katz and Tush,* or all three, briefly talk about the power that stories hold for the main characters. Then let children become storytellers themselves. Encourage them to ask special older friends, neighbors, or grandparents to relate tales from childhood or to retell stories they heard when they were children. Students might pick a favorite story and ask for permission to share it with the class. After practicing the story, the children can tell it to a small group of classmates. If children feel comfortable with a larger audience, they might invite the original storytellers to hear their tales retold to the entire class.

To extend the activity, look for local storytelling professionals or an amateur storytellers' group. Invite a representative to the classroom. Let children take turns with the storyteller and share a fine afternoon "swapping yarns."

Activities of the Heart: Building Citizenship Dispositions

ACTIVITY 1. After reading *Uncle Willie and the Soup Kitchen,* talk with students about how Willie and his nephew **help the needy**. Let children describe the ways in which they have assisted people and the results of these efforts. Then brainstorm social concerns in your neighborhood or community and realistic ways that children could help deal with them. List these possible relief projects on the chalkboard, overhead, or on butcher paper.

To extend this activity, the class might consider their list and identify a project of particular concern, such as visiting a nursing home regularly, supporting relief efforts for disaster victims, or collecting canned goods for a food bank. Recruit an older volunteer to serve as project consultant, enabling the class to reach its goal by the end of the school year.

ACTIVITY 2. To **foster respect across generations**, help children sense how age influences the things that people can do. Encourage them to recognize that many older people have trouble performing tasks that younger people take for granted (e.g., arthritis sufferers might have difficulty tying shoelaces). Read stories that show people of different ages attempting and accomplishing simple tasks, such as *Just Like Max, Grandma's Baseball, Island Boy, The Memory Box,* and *Mr. Jordan in the Park.*

Ask children to think about the relative ease with which certain characters completed various chores. On a large mural, have them draw things people can do at different ages and write brief captions for their illustrations. At one end of the mural, students should picture things a 1-year-old can do, then a 5-year-old, then a 10-year-old, continuing in five-year increments. As they work on the mural, children might ask people of varying ages what they can comfortably accomplish, adding these examples as appropriate.

Once the artwork is completed, have children compare and contrast what different age levels can typically accomplish. Guide them to an awareness that these accomplishments are not bad or deserving of ridicule, but different and deserving of understanding, and oftentimes respect.

ACTIVITY 3. Develop children's **sensitivity to the effects of anger** as you read aloud selected stories, such as *What Kind of Babysitter Is This?, The Day of the Rainbow,* or *Grandma's Baseball.* Generate a list of factors that make characters angry in these stories. Ask the children to talk to older friends or relatives about the kinds of things that make them angry and add these new ideas to the list.

Using examples from the stories, discuss ways that people show their anger. What happens when angry people react inappropriately? Brainstorm appropriate ways to deal with angry feelings. Let the class decide how best to illustrate these suggestions for sharing with other groups of students (e.g., puppetry, role-playing, large pictures, illustrations on an overhead projector).

Section 2

Diversity in Terms of Gender Roles—
Venturing Beyond
Traditional Roles

To broaden and deepen their appreciation for diversity, young children should explore other types of relationships besides the intergenerational. Teachers and librarians must also help children respect their own uniqueness, value the special qualities of peers, and accept the traditional and nontraditional roles that Americans assume with increasing frequency. Through literature, we can show children that they have every right to be themselves, as long as they respect that same right for others (chapter 4). We can show young people that boys and girls can achieve more than "peaceful coexistence"; they might even enjoy wonderful friendships that cross traditional sex-role boundaries (chapter 5). We can help children recognize that assuming nontraditional social and job roles can yield challenging and meaningful experiences (chapter 6). As they venture beyond customary expectations, boys and girls can gain the wisdom, skills, and attitudes for demonstrating civic competence.

Chapter 4

Being Yourself—
The Choice Is Up to You

This chapter conveys an important citizenship principle—every individual has the right to become whomever he or she wants to be. All too often, peer pressure and social expectations force children to abandon unusual aspirations and to hide unique personal gifts. For a girl to play baseball, or a boy to have dolls, or a boy and a girl to become best friends, young people must believe that they possess or have a chance to develop the ability as well as the right to enter and leave whatever experiences they might choose.

The stories cited in this chapter present examples of children overcoming opposition and gaining self-confidence as they pursue what they like to do best. In the feature title, *Amazing Grace*, a talented, vital girl ignores nay-sayers, practices hard, gets the lead role in the class play, and gives a dazzling performance as Peter Pan. The many alternate and related titles can open additional pathways for student learning.

Feature Title

Amazing Grace by Mary Hoffman. Illus. by Caroline Binch. New York: Dial Press, 1991. 32p. ISBN 0-803-71040-2.

Grace loves to read, hear, and make up stories, and her imagination allows her to bring any character to life. When her teacher announces that the class will perform *Peter Pan*, Grace quickly casts herself in the title role. Though classmates chide her that she cannot play Peter Pan because she is black and a girl, Grace convinces everyone that she *is* Peter and wows the opening-night audience.

Hoffman's book introduces many citizenship dispositions, opportunities to build interpersonal skills, and lessons about human motivation. In particular, Grace is a strong female role model who finds something that she wants very much, works hard to achieve that goal, and, by her example, prompts classmates to do their best.

Alternate Titles

Daddy Has a Pair of Striped Shorts by Mimi Otey. New York: Farrar, Straus & Giroux, 1990. 36p. ISBN 0-374-31675-9.

A girl and her brother find their father's style of dress most embarrassing. Eventually, they agree that appearance may not be everything; loving, helping, and caring for people are often more valuable qualities than dressing "to a T."

Daddy demonstrates important social studies concepts by asserting his right to dress as he pleases. Students might recognize the importance of self-esteem and discover that expressing individuality is one way to build a positive sense of self. They might also value positive social interaction and find opportunities to practice human relations skills.

Regina's Big Mistake by Marissa Moss. Boston: Houghton Mifflin, 1990. 28p. ISBN 0-395-55330-X.

Regina is drawing a jungle and it is not going well. She compares her own artwork to her classmates' and gets more and more frustrated. Finally, she pauses, thinks about what needs doing, and transforms a messy mistake into an attractive piece of artwork.

As they examine Regina's multicultural classroom, readers cannot help but consider important ideas that directly influence the practice of citizenship. The story illustrates the power of constructive, as opposed to negative, criticism and lets students compare and contrast different ways that individuals might approach a similar task.

William's Doll by Charlotte Zolotow. Illus. by Robert Pène du Bois. New York: HarperCollins, 1972. 30p. ISBN 0-060-27048-9.

Though William really likes "boy things" such as playing trains and basketball, deep down inside he wants a doll. Nobody listens to his unusual request. Finally, his grandmother grants his wish, noting that caring for a doll can help even the toughest and roughest boy to be a good father.

Zolotow's classic story suggests classroom experiences that can reinforce important social studies learnings. First, young readers might realize that understanding another's viewpoint is critical to positive social interaction. Second, children might be motivated to play with all kinds of toys—one way to promote their self-esteem and self-confidence.

Related Titles

All I Am by Eileen Roe. Illus. by Helen Cogancherry. New York: Bradbury Press, 1990. 24p. ISBN 0-027-77372-8.

A small boy tells what he is now—helper, friend, and stargazer. At the same time, he finds himself wondering what he will be when he grows up.

The Art Lesson by Tomie dePaola. New York: Putnam, 1989. 32p. ISBN 0-399-21688-X.

Throughout kindergarten and first grade, Tommy's frustration mounts in art class. He doesn't want to just sit and listen. One day, a sensitive art teacher gives him a chance to express his emotions to the world.

Bear's Picture by Daniel Pinkwater. New York: Dutton Children's Books, 1984. 32p. ISBN 0-525-44102-6.

Even after "two fine gentlemen" criticize his painting, Bear remains content with his artwork, because it reflects what he feels inside.

Cleversticks by Bernard Ashley. Illus. by Derek Brazell. New York: Crown, 1992. 32p. ISBN 0-517-58879-X.

Ling Sung struggles with the little things that his classmates do so easily. His spirits lift when they cannot match his skill with chopsticks, no matter how hard they try.

Elmer by David McKee. New York: Lothrop, Lee & Shepard, 1989. 32p. ISBN 0-688-09172-5.

All the elephants are gray except Elmer, whose skin is a patchwork of many colors. Elmer wants so much to be like everyone else until he realizes that his colorful nature lets him fill a key role in the elephant community.

Harry's Helicopter by Joan Anderson. Photos by George Ancona. New York: Morrow Junior Books, 1990. 32p. ISBN 0-688-09186-5.

For his birthday, Harry receives a red cardboard helicopter from his father. During an imaginary ride over New York City, Harry's fantasy turns very, very real!

Jenny by Beth P. Wilson. Illus. by Dolores Johnson. New York: Macmillan, 1990. 32p. ISBN 0-027-93120-X.

Jenny's poetry conveys her musings and wonderings about her extended family, holidays, and friends.

Just Us Women by Jeannette Franklin Caines. Illus. by Pat Cummings. New York: HarperCollins, 1982. 32p. ISBN 0-060-20942-9.

A young black girl and her favorite aunt plan an enjoyable, leisurely car trip to North Carolina, without any men to bother them.

Neighborhood Trucker by Louise Borden. Illus. by Sandra Speidel. New York: Scholastic, 1990. 32p. ISBN 0-590-42584-6.

Elliott spends much of his time indulging his fascination with trucks, especially the cement mixers from the concrete plant near his home. As he watches, he dreams of the day when he will drive his own 18-wheeler.

Shoes from Grandpa by Mem Fox. Illus. by Patricia Mullins. New York: Orchard, 1990, c1989. 32p. ISBN 0-531-08448-5.

Lots of proper folks try to give Jessie just the right clothes to go with her new shoes. Tactfully, she insists that she would rather wear jeans.

What Mary Jo Shared by Janice May Udry. Illus. by Eleanor Mill. Morton Grove, IL: A. Whitman, 1966. 40p. ISBN 0-807-58842-3.

Everyone in the class has brought something to share, but Mary Jo cannot locate just the right something. A unique idea hits her one day—why not bring her father to show and tell?

Willie's Not the Hugging Kind by Joyce Durham Barrett. Illus. by Pat Cummings. New York: Harper & Row, 1989. 32p. ISBN 0-060-20417-6.

A young African-American boy is in a quandary about whether or not to hug family members. Willie still likes the idea, but his Asian friend argues that hugging is for sissies. Ultimately, he works out a compromise that leaves most everyone smiling.

Teaching Options

The following activities can be introduced after reading *Amazing Grace* or alternate or related titles. Because most involve children's emotions and could uncover personal situations, adjust particular activities as classroom circumstances dictate. Remember: Using multiple books to generate an activity lets children examine feelings from different angles and through varied lenses.

Activities of the Head: Building Citizenship Understandings

ACTIVITY 1. After-school activities with friends can help children develop interpersonal skills and improve their self-confidence. After reading selected titles, such as *Amazing Grace*, *All I Am*, *The Art Lesson*, *The Neighborhood Trucker*, or *Harry's Helicopter*, ask students to **consider the benefits that group participation can bring**. Briefly discuss what selected characters in these stories choose to do with friends after school (e.g., gymnastics, art projects, sports, dance, drama). Prompt students to list what they find appealing about each group activity. Then initiate and guide a dialogue in which children examine their motivations for trying similar after-school experiences. Do they weigh the benefits that a particular form of group participation might provide? Or are they swayed by other factors, such as peer pressure or parental command, when choosing to play sports or attend a dance class? Why might they abandon an experience that brings many benefits? What sports or games might be worth trying for the first time?

For enrichment, have each student make a name tag that indicates her or his favorite group activity and arrange for children in a neighboring classroom to do the same. Let everyone mill around together searching for new interests, for something they have never tried before, perhaps because they labeled it a "girl thing" or a "boy thing." Have children recruit a coach who can teach needed skills. Provide time for groups to meet and enjoy their new interests. Repeat the process as many times as possible so that students learn several new pastimes they might enjoy with others.

ACTIVITY 2. To **encourage global awareness**, ask children to investigate after-school games and sports that are popular in other nations. Group students, then let each group choose a country and, with assistance from parent volunteers and your school librarian, search for information about the sports and games favored there. After groups share their findings, class members can categorize sports and games as similar to or different from the ones in which they regularly participate. Help students determine characteristics common to after-school activities at home and abroad and decide which they would most like to play.

With assistance from your school's PE teacher or music teacher or both, pick several "foreign" sports and games for which students have expressed a preference. Teach these activities in PE classes or music classes or both, and encourage children to continue playing them at recess and to teach them to family members.

ACTIVITY 3. Toys are tools for building confidence and skills. This activity helps young children **realize that personal preferences need not depend on the whims of others, and that variety really is the spice of life**. After reading such stories as *William's Doll, Jenny, Harry's Helicopter, Amazing Grace, All I Am,* or *Neighborhood Trucker*, have children list two or three favorite toys on index cards of two different colors (please—not pink and blue!). Boys should use one color and girls the other color. Collect the cards and help small groups categorize them by type, such as dolls, blocks, Legos, and vehicles. Next, groups can determine which toys in each category were named most often by girls and which were named most often by boys, and graph the results. In a large group discussion, help students draw some conclusions about these results, particularly why some categories seemed to be boy toys and others seemed to be girl toys.

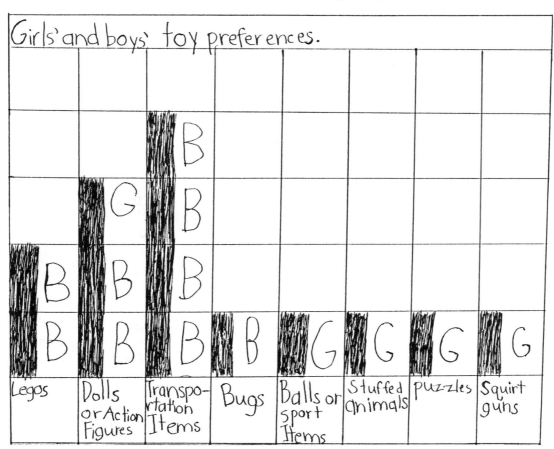

Fig. 4. A bar graph showing girls' and boys' toy preferences. *(Graph by Joshua Betts, age 9. Data from Andy McGowan, age 5, Molly Workman, age 5, Claire McGowan, age 7, and Joshua Betts)*

To build older students' **written communication skills**, ask pairs or trios to write items and compile a questionnaire to elicit toy preference information. Give the survey to students in other classrooms and compare the results.

ACTIVITY 4. The examples of several chapter 4 characters **introduce children to the limitations imposed by gender stereotyping**. For example, Grace hears that she cannot be Peter Pan because she is a girl. Because they are boys, William is repeatedly told that he cannot have a doll and Willie that he cannot hug family members. Read one or more chapter 4 stories aloud, then encourage children to brainstorm additional examples of the ways in which stereotyping might prevent them from developing important skills and self-confidence. Discuss the validity of assumptions about student performance, such as "only boys can play ball," "girls can't do math," "big boys don't cry," and "girls cook and clean."

After compiling the list, let small groups of boys and girls converse about ways to discourage these attitudes and lift the restrictions they often impose. These dialogues could lead children to practice and improve their abilities to perform tasks and study subject areas that they previously thought were taboo. Ask children to write their reactions to these discussions and the self-improvement sessions in their journals.

Activities of the Hand: Building Citizenship Skills

ACTIVITY 1. Children need practice **building skills to communicate ideas and participate in classroom conversation**. They also need to **develop the personal pride that sharing accomplishments can bring**. After reading *Cleversticks*, *Regina's Big Mistake*, *The Art Lesson*, *What Mary Jo Shared*, or all of these, ask students to pick a favorite playtime hobby, such as playing the piano, drawing trucks, building with Legos, and singing along to records. Then help volunteers plan a mini-lesson to teach their tasks to a small group of classmates or to the whole class if they feel comfortable. As they plan, show young teachers how to break down playtime activities into necessary skills and describe these competencies in sequence. Encourage them to share how they practice and improve their skills as well as the joy they get from performing them well. If your students cannot manage mini-lessons, scale down the activity to a show-and-tell session in which children demonstrate something that they do very well.

ACTIVITY 2. In *Just Us Women*, a girl and her aunt plan and take "just the right kind of trip" to North Carolina. In *Harry's Helicopter*, a boy takes a fantasy ride over New York City. After sharing these and other trip stories with the class, small groups of students could **sharpen their map skills** by locating where these travels occurred relative to their home town and sharing their findings (e.g., "North Carolina is right *here* on the map, and it's east of where we live").

Pairs or trios of older primary students could extend this activity by planning and plotting their own dream trips on state, national, or world maps.

Activities of the Heart: Building Citizenship Dispositions

ACTIVITY 1. This activity encourages students to **acknowledge their own positive attitudes and abilities as well as those of classmates**. Several chapter 4 titles, especially *Bear's Picture, Elmer, Daddy Has a Pair of Striped Shorts,* and *Amazing Grace,* introduce and support this exercise. To begin, give children pieces of butcher paper and help them trace their bodies in crayon. Allow them to use various media, including poster paints, if classroom conditions and your courage permit, to add detail and personality to their body sketches. As they discover strengths during the year, have children draw or write directly on their illustrations about positive qualities, activities they can do, and new skills they can perform. As familiarity and trust grow, let children add comments and pictures to each other's body sketches, with prior permission, of course.

Use the body drawings as hall or wall decorations and as yardsticks of student growth and development over the year.

ACTIVITY 2. To parallel the previous activity, a teacher or librarian could place a large sheet of paper on the wall and challenge students to catch classmates or friends **saying kind words or doing good things for others**. When a student catches someone being kind or doing good, she or he writes that person's name with a brief description or drawing of the positive words or deeds, or both. Continue until the chart is full. Periodically, discuss the feelings that the chart generates and consider the implications of saying and doing good. Because it focuses on constructive versus negative criticism, *Regina's Big Mistake* is a natural to introduce this activity.

ACTIVITY 3. Just as the small boy in *All I Am* wonders what he will become, students are **testing the basic attitudes and values** that will influence their lives as citizens. Using *All I Am* as a springboard, ask children to draw jobs and hobbies that they wish to learn as they grow up. Form small groups with similar interests, then bring in role models knowledgeable and skillful in these vocations and avocations. Guests should speak about the training and equipment required to pursue these interests. They should also discuss the attitudes and values necessary to be proficient in their occupations and pastimes. List these qualities on the chalkboard, overhead, or butcher paper and discuss them with students. Develop a short list of attitudes and values that seem to be universals and post them in your classroom.

Chapter 5

Making and Keeping Friends—
Boys and Girls Together

Our fifth chapter advances an idea that will seem heretical to a first- or second-grader—that boys and girls can have lasting friendships with members of the opposite sex. The literature selections present many situations in which girls and boys look beyond gender lines, develop rewarding friendships, and learn to appreciate the adage about not judging a book by its cover, or a person by clothing style or athletic ability. Because it so clearly exemplifies the chapter theme, our feature title is Elizabeth Winthrop's *Lizzie and Harold*. Fourteen additional titles reinforce the notion that girls and boys can be friends and extend many options for teaching and learning.

Feature Title

Lizzie and Harold by Elizabeth Winthrop. Illus. by Martha Weston. New York: Lothrop, Lee & Shepard, 1986. 32p. ISBN 0-688-02712-1.

In her search for the perfect companion, Lizzie quickly discounts boys, because, as we all know, a boy can never be a girl's best friend. Eventually, Lizzie realizes that Harold might make a wonderful companion. Harold lives next door, Lizzie enjoys his company, and his frequent visits suggest that he kind of likes hanging around her, too!

Winthrop examines the sometimes rocky road to boy-girl friendships in a familiar, personal way. The story, moreover, encourages students to identify meaningful attributes for friendship and to consider the feelings, both positive and painful, that friendships can generate.

Alternate Titles

Horrible Harry's Secret by Suzy Kline. New York: Viking, 1990. 52p. ISBN 0-670-82470-4.

In the second grade, any friendship can sometimes try the patience of even the most agreeable young man, let alone Horrible Harry. Imagine Horrible's distress when Song Lee brings her water frog to show and tell one morning, and he finds himself fascinated by her—getting friendly with a girl, no less!

In sharing sessions, primary children can relate their personal experiences to Horrible Harry's dilemma and discover important knowledge about friendship. The book also suggests opportunities for sharpening social-studies skills like information gathering and critical thinking, and for discussing subjects such as divorce and the Korean War.

Jamaica Tag-Along by Juanita Havill. Illus. by Anne S. O'Brien. Boston: Houghton Mifflin, 1989. 30p. ISBN 0-395-49602-0.

Jamaica's older brother refuses to let her play basketball. Angry at Ossie, Jamaica then mistreats Berto when he tries to have fun with her on the playground. Realizing that Berto's feelings have been hurt badly, Jamaica decides to practice what she has preached to Ossie. She joins Berto in the sandbox and completes a serious engineering project!

Havill's engaging story can help children understand the emotions that influence our interactions with others and make friendship such a precious commodity. The book also introduces activities that promote important citizenship competencies, such as oral communication, interpersonal relations, and perceiving other points of view.

Julian's Glorious Summer by Ann Cameron. Illus. by Dora Leder. New York: Random House, 1987. 64p. ISBN 0-394-99117-6.

Gloria wants Julian to ride bikes with her in the neighborhood. Afraid to ride his bike, but unwilling to admit his reluctance to a girl, Julian tells her that he is too busy. When his father discovers the lie, he assigns so much work that Julian really is too busy!

Reading about Julian and Gloria can help students identify essential aspects of productive relationships, such as honesty, openness, and trust. In decision-making exercises, students might also compare and contrast how they would have handled Julian's situation and propose alternative solutions.

Related Titles

Anna's Secret Friend by Yoriko Tsutsui. Illus. by Akiko Hayashi. New York: Puffin Books, 1989. 31p. ISBN 0-140-50731-0.

Soon after moving to a new place, Anna finds secret gifts on her doorstep. She finally catches a girl leaving another gift and the two strike up a friendship.

Chicken Sunday by Patricia Polacco. New York: Philomel, 1992. 32p. ISBN 0-399-22133-6.

Three friends—two boys and a girl—hatch a plot to obtain a new Easter hat for the boys' grandmother.

Daniel's Dog by Jo Ellen Bogart. Illus. by Janet Wilson. New York: Scholastic, 1990. 32p. ISBN 0-590-43402-0.

A young boy named Norman and his imaginary dog, Lucy, help a young African-American boy adjust to the arrival of a new baby sister.

Don't Be My Valentine by Joan M. Lexau. Illus. by Syd Hoff. New York: HarperCollins, 1985. 64p. ISBN 0-060-23873-9.

Sam makes a mean valentine for Amy Lou, but somehow it is delivered to his teacher instead. Eventually, he and his friends explain everything.

Everett Anderson's Friend by Lucille Clifton. Illus. by Ann Grifalconi. New York: Henry Holt, 1992. 24p. ISBN 0-805-02246-5.

When Everett discovers that a family of girls is moving in next door, his first reaction is negative. He soon discovers that Maria is fun to play with after all.

I'm Calling Molly by Jane Kurtz. Illus. by Irene Trivas. Morton Grove, IL: A. Whitman, 1990. 32p. ISBN 0-807-53468-4.

Christopher, a four-year-old with newly acquired telephone skills, calls his friend, Molly, to ask if she can play. Frustrated at first, because she is busy with another friend, he is elated when she finally calls him back and agrees to play.

My Cousin Charlie by Phyllis Root. Illus. by Pia Marella. Milwaukee, WI: Raintree, 1985. 32p. ISBN 0-940-74240-3.

Rita visits her cousin Charlie, but he refuses to let her play with his baseball because she is a girl. When he comes to play at her house later, she gives him a dose of his own medicine.

Playing Marbles by Julie Brinckloe. New York: Morrow Junior Books, 1988. 32p. ISBN 0-688-07144-9.

A girl proves her skill at marbles, opening the door for friendship with two boys.

Stevie by John Steptoe. New York: HarperCollins, 1969. 24p. ISBN 0-060-25764-4.

Robert wishes that Stevie would leave. After he is gone, Robert realizes how much fun they had together.

Three Wishes by Lucille Clifton. Illus. by Michael Hays. New York: Doubleday, 1992. 32p. ISBN 0-385-30497-8.

Finding a lucky penny, Nobie makes three wishes on it. The result is an argument that ruins her friendship with Victorius. After a heart-to-heart with her mother, Nobie wishes that she "still had a good friend."

Yo! Yes? by Chris Raschka. New York: Orchard, 1993. 32p. ISBN 0-531-08619-4.

With few words spoken, two boys, one white and one black, meet on the street and decide to play together.

Teaching Options

After reading *Lizzie and Harold* or any of the alternate or related stories, introduce one or more of the following activities. Though not intended for use with specific titles, activities may work better with some books than others. As we have suggested in previous chapters, please modify any teaching idea to suit your classroom situation and consider incorporating multiple titles in particular activities.

Activities of the Head: Building Citizenship Understandings

ACTIVITY 1. In most primary classrooms, teachers help children **understand the benefits of positive social interaction.** A major aspect of that understanding, **knowing the essential qualities of friendship,** is the focus for this activity. After reading *Lizzie and Harold, My Cousin Charlie, Chicken Sunday, Yo! Yes?,* or *Everett Anderson's Friend,* let pairs or trios brainstorm what it is that makes someone a good friend, then share their conclusions in a large group. Compile a master list of these qualities on the board. Help students recognize that their list holds true for boy-boy, girl-girl, and even girl-boy relationships.

Guided by these understandings, children can create a poster or collage of magazine pictures, photos from home, or drawings that show the many ways in which people demonstrate friendship and the many benefits that they gain from personal relationships.

ACTIVITY 2. *Julian's Glorious Summer* and *Jamaica Tag-Along* illustrate **how important communication can be and how people can work to improve its effectiveness.** After sharing one or both of these stories, pair children, preferably in boy-girl combinations, and have them role-play a conversation about a recent classroom event. After the role players have concluded, reconvene the large group and ask children to identify factors that helped or hindered their attempts to communicate. On a large sheet of butcher paper, generate a class list of factors that promote effective communication. As children share ideas, lead them to the conclusion that people who live in the same household or work in the same classroom must communicate. Although interaction can be difficult, people can improve the flow of ideas by observing certain rules. After the discussion, have children illustrate the class list with examples of people interacting productively and post it in a visible classroom location.

ACTIVITY 3. To follow up activity 2, give students a chance to **compare and contrast how to arrive at workable solutions to communication problems**. Reread *Julian's Glorious Summer* or *Jamaica Tag-Along* paying particular attention to the ways in which the main characters interact. Divide children into small groups, each with three or four members, including both girls and boys, and ask them to select a situation in which the characters have difficulty communicating. Give each group a charge: Examine this instance of miscommunication carefully and determine the nature of the problem, who or what is causing it, and what the characters do to address it. Have groups share their findings in a whole-class discussion.

Ph.3. Children working in small groups. *(Lindsey McMahan, Jada Sullivan)*

To extend this activity, return students to small groups. Direct them to consider the severity of the problems they have identified and the relative merits of the attempts to solve them. Then have each small group develop another way to narrow the communication gap that might work even better than the characters' original approach. In a whole-class setting, each group can propose and defend its alternative solution.

Activities of the Hand: Building Citizenship Skills

ACTIVITY 1. This activity boosts children's ability to **organize and visually display information** as well as their **understanding that change is a constant in our lives**. While reading *Daniel's Dog* aloud, help children recognize that Daniel's life has changed dramatically. As children discuss the story, guide them to the awareness that everything changes over time, even personal relationships, and that friends can ease the rough spots that often accompany life's many transformations.

So children can apply these understandings, let them create timelines displaying significant changes that they, their friends, or families have experienced over the past year. Children can construct their timelines from personal photos, magazine or newspaper clippings, and drawings. To reinforce these understandings, children can also make bar and line graphs that show their heights, weights, homework habits, family sizes, personal possessions, or other statistical changes over time.

ACTIVITY 2. As our chapter titles illustrate, strong friendships, even boy-girl relationships, can continue and prosper across great distances. To **build map and globe skills**, ask students to identify close friends or family members who live far away—people whom they care about but rarely see. On a large map or globe, if appropriate, have children locate these individuals using push-pins, markers, or tape. In a class discussion, briefly compare and contrast these locations (e.g., whose friend lives closest to our town? farthest away? how many live in Europe? in Asia? in Africa? would you use a plane, train, car, or boat to reach this friend?).

To **hone written communication skills**, ask children to select one long-lost friend or family member and write him or her a letter. Depending on children's writing abilities, you may need to review the elements of a friendly letter or secure older students to assist younger writers. Assign helpers across gender lines, if possible.

ACTIVITY 3. Chapter 5 titles suggest many opportunities to **foster the skills and dispositions for working cooperatively**. In these stories, boys and girls are separated and united by various circumstances. For example, the ability to ride a bicycle comes between Julian and Gloria (*Julian's Glorious Summer*); obtaining an Easter hat brings two boys and a girl together (*Chicken Sunday*). Valentines cause a rift in Sam and Amy Lou's class (*Don't Be My Valentine*); marbles (*Playing Marbles*) and baseball (*My Cousin Charlie*) open positive girl-boy friendships.

Read-aloud as many of these stories as time permits, then compare and contrast them with your class. As the discussion proceeds, focus conversation on the activities that generated difficulties between boys and girls. Let students determine whether any seem gender specific (e.g., "boys are naturally poor bicycle riders") or whether any seem disagreement prone (e.g., "kids always fight when they give valentines"). Lead students to the observation that none of these activities is restricted to either boys or girls and that none must inevitably create conflict.

Then form cooperative work groups, each with three or four boys and girls, and ask each team to prepare an argument that play activities are neither gender specific nor disagreement prone. To gather evidence, older children may use reference materials and interview experts by themselves, and younger ones might need more assistance. Conclude by having the teams present their arguments to the entire class; let students assess why particular arguments seemed effective.

Activities of the Heart: Building Citizenship Dispositions

ACTIVITY 1. To raise students' awareness that **positive and negative feelings can influence our behavior**, read one or more of these titles aloud: *Jamaica Tag-Along, Playing Marbles, Stevie, Julian's Glorious Summer, Three Wishes, Don't Be My Valentine*. Then talk with children about the emotions that story characters might feel, and help them make a list of negative and positive "feeling words." After students demonstrate a sense of these emotions and their impact, form boy-girl pairs and assign each partnership one of the following situations to role-play:

1. how you behave around people who show positive feelings;
2. how you behave around people who show negative feelings;
3. how you talk with someone who is showing positive feelings;
4. how negative feelings, when they arise, can change our behavior;
5. how you let someone know that he or she has hurt your feelings.

As you discuss the role plays with the class, focus on the ways that negative and positive feelings influence our behavior toward others.

ACTIVITY 2. Throughout our lives we form many human relationships, some short-term and others that are long-lasting. This activity encourages children to examine relationships to **discover attitudes and values that draw one friend to another**. After reading a recommended story aloud, ask children to talk to a friend or a relative whom they particularly like, especially a member of the opposite sex. Encourage students to investigate what prompted these relationships and what encourages them to flourish. Working in pairs or trios, the children might pool their information, draw conclusions, and present their findings to classmates in an engaging manner.

ACTIVITY 3. Valuing friends and family is an important citizenship disposition. Help children appreciate interpersonal relationships by identifying "warm fuzzies" (positive reinforcement like hugs or smiles) that they regularly receive from friends and relatives, especially across gender lines. Consider sharing *Anna's Secret Friend,* or *Chicken Sunday,* or both, because these titles illustrate the delivery and impact of many warm fuzzies. Chart phrases or actions that students can use to **build the self-esteem of significant people in their lives.**

To conclude, challenge each student to set a personal goal—delivering five warm fuzzies each day for one week. Warm fuzzy targets must include at least one classmate of the opposite sex. As enrichment, ask children to draw pictures or write stories illustrating the extent to which they met this goal; provide time for them to discuss the impact of these positive phrases.

Chapter 6

Performing Nontraditional Roles—
The Policewoman and Mr. Mom

Chapter 6 introduces and examines the notion that assuming nontraditional roles can be socially important as well as personally challenging. Characters in this chapter's story selections perform tasks and assume attitudes considered nontraditional by some. Teachers, librarians, and students should enjoy examining out-of-the-ordinary people and the reactions that they sometimes generate. Admittedly, a story in which the mother takes a job outside the home may seem fairly traditional in the 1990s. Still, our feature title allows children to personalize and make meaning from the chapter theme. The alternate and related titles expand the notion of "Officer Ms. and Mr. Mom" in new and intriguing directions.

Feature Title

The Terrible Thing That Happened at Our House by Marge Blaine. Illus. by John Wallner. New York: Four Winds Press, 1984. Reprint of 1975 ed. 33p. ISBN 0-027-10720-5.

Two youngsters react badly to lifestyle changes that result when their mother takes a job outside the home. Everyone starts rushing around; school lunches replace sandwiches in a sack; and no one has time for reading, stories, and fun. Fortunately, family members air their feelings and work out ways to return things closer to "normal."

Though an older title, this book examines social studies skills that are relevant today. For example, children need to understand the feelings and attitudes of others; they must distinguish between wants and needs; they should be able to work together to solve problems; and they should be willing to assume new family roles, if necessary.

Alternate Titles

Daddy Makes the Best Spaghetti by Anna Grossnickle Hines. New York: Clarion Books, 1986. 32p. ISBN 0-899-19388-9.

With the mom working outside the home, the father and son spend time doing things together, like cooking a mouth-watering spaghetti sauce that the whole family can enjoy.

Hines's story elaborates crucial citizenship dispositions like facing responsibility, sharing talents, accommodating change, and enjoying a sense of accomplishment. The book also suggests experiences that enable young people to acquire and apply citizenship skills, particularly the ability to make decisions, solve problems, and work cooperatively and collaboratively.

The Long Red Scarf by Nette Hilton. Illus. by Margaret Power. Minneapolis, MN: Carolrhoda Books, 1990, c1987. 32p. ISBN 0-876-14399-0.

Grandpa admires his friend's knitted scarf so much that he tries to persuade several family members to make one for him. After hearing the reply "I'm busy" too many times, Grandpa knits his own scarf, with Cousin Izzy providing technical assistance.

Hilton's humorous story encourages children to apply several social studies skills. First, whether he needed a warm scarf or just wanted one, Grandpa handled a personal problem by learning a new skill, one not often associated with grandfatherly figures. Second, the story's setting provides an opportunity for students to compare and contrast various climates as well as the lifestyles that different weather patterns demand.

Three Strong Women: A Tall Tale from Japan by Claus Stamm. Illus. by Jean Tseng and Mou-sien Tseng. New York: Viking, 1990. 32p. ISBN 0-670-83323-1.

By retelling a Japanese folktale, Maru-me, her mother, and her grandmother teach a famous wrestler, Forever Mountain, two powerful lessons: A person's real strength has little to do with muscle size, and humility might just be the greatest virtue.

This tale supports the primary social studies curriculum in a number of ways. The characters in Stamm's book are larger than life, providing children with the opportunity to interpret and predict their sometimes outrageous actions and to compare and contrast them with mortal folk. Children might also examine Stamm's view of Japanese culture in terms of more realistic stories about Japan, such as *How My Parents Learned to Eat* by Ina R. Friedman (Houghton Mifflin, 1987). Other books include *Bicycle Man* by Allen Say (Parnassus Press, 1982), and *The Park Bench* by Fumi Takeshita (Kane/Miller, 1988).

Related Titles

Baseball Ballerina by Kathryn Cristaldi. Illus. by Abby Carter. New York: Random House, 1992. 48p. ISBN 0-679-91734-9.

In this very funny book, a girl who loves to play baseball finds herself taking a ballet class against her will. She and her friend keep ballet a secret so that their teammates on the Sharks will not laugh at them. The secret lasts until an unusual plot twist makes ballet much more acceptable.

Bea and Mr. Jones by Amy Schwartz. New York: Bradbury Press, 1982. ISBN 0-027-81430-0.

Bea, a kindergartner, and her father, an office worker, generate some interesting consequences when they decide to trade "jobs."

Justin and the Best Biscuits in the World by Mildred Pitts Walter. Illus. by Catherine Stock. New York: Lothrop, Lee & Shepard, 1986. 122p. ISBN 0-688-06645-3.

In this longer but very listenable story, Justin has a tough time living in a house full of females who insist that he do "women's work." While visiting his grandfather's ranch, he discovers that he-men cowboys cook and clean, too.

Just Us Women by Jeannette Franklin Caines. Illus. by Pat Cummings. New York: HarperCollins, 1982. 32p. ISBN 0-060-20942-9.

An African-American girl and her favorite aunt plan an enjoyable, leisurely car trip to North Carolina without any men to bother them.

Katie Morag and the Two Grandmothers by Mairi Hedderwick. Boston: Little, Brown, 1986. 25p. ISBN 0-316-35400-7.

Katie is amazed by her two grandmothers: Granny Island, a rough-and-tumble farmer, and Granny Mainland, a dainty, proper lady. By story's end, Katie realizes that they are not strong and weak or good and bad, just very different from each other.

The Man Who Kept House by Kathleen Hague and Michael Hague. Illus. by Michael Hague. San Diego, CA: Harcourt Brace Jovanovich, 1981. 32p. ISBN 0-152-51698-0.

Convinced that his work in the fields is more difficult than his wife's house-work, a farmer trades places with her for a day—a day that becomes synonymous with disaster!

Mr. Nick's Knitting by Margaret Wild. Illus. by Dee H. Huxley. San Diego, CA: Harcourt Brace Jovanovich, 1989. 32p. ISBN 0-152-00518-8.

Mr. Nick and Mrs. Jolley might seem quite an abnormal sight as they knit together while traveling into the city by train. When Mrs. Jolley becomes ill, Mr. Nick responds in a very normal manner—he knits a special gift to lift his friend's spirits.

No, Agatha by Rachel Isadora. New York: Greenwillow Books, 1980. 32p. ISBN 0-688-84274-7.

Agatha is aboard a ship bound for Europe in 1908, but every time she tries to do something that she might enjoy, like climbing or running, someone tells her "No!" Not yet ready to behave like a lady, Agatha grows increasingly frustrated by turn-of-the-century conventions.

Roses Sing on New Snow: A Delicious Tale by Paul Yee. Illus. by Harvey Chan. New York: Macmillan, 1991. 32p. ISBN 0-027-93622-8.

In Chinatown during the early 1900s, Maylin is the primary cook in her father's restaurant. To her distress, her brothers receive all the credit. When a government official asks that a favorite dish be prepared in his presence, the truth finally emerges.

Sam Johnson and the Blue Ribbon Quilt by Lisa Campbell Ernst. New York: Lothrop, Lee & Shepard, 1983. 32p. ISBN 0-688-01517-4.

While mending the pig pen awning, Sam discovers that he really enjoys sewing. However, when he asks his wife if he can join her quilting club, he finds ridicule rather than acceptance.

Teaching Options

After sharing *The Terrible Thing That Happened at Our House* or another of the preceding titles, incorporate one or more of the following activities into your teaching. Though most activities need not feature a specific title, they may work better with some stories than with others. Teaching ideas can also be modified as your needs dictate. We hope that you can expand your options by including multiple titles to enrich particular activities.

Activities of the Head: Building Citizenship Understandings

ACTIVITY 1. This activity assists children in **reexamining male and female roles.** Many jobs once considered gender specific are being performed by both women and men, such as nursing, housekeeping, police work, and flying aircraft. Read one or more titles that illustrate switches in male and female roles. After reviewing the story or stories, invite parents or other community members with nontraditional jobs to talk with the class; be sure to encourage children to ask questions of their guests. Afterwards, have students make a list of jobs that could be filled by either men or women. Then revise the initial lists as necessary.

To follow up, review the nontraditional roles on the revised lists. Ask each class member to prioritize the top five jobs that she or he would like to perform some day. Let each child illustrate his or her top choice using a favorite art medium.

ACTIVITY 2. In this activity, children **gather information and gain new insights about the role of the working mom**. After reading *The Terrible Thing That Happened at Our House*, *The Man Who Kept House*, or related titles, let children dialogue about being a working mom; encourage them to relate personal experiences to situations described in the stories. Confirm and extend their new understandings by inviting several working moms to tea with small groups of students. Try to find nontraditional role models, but invite at least one housekeeper. As part of each gathering, videotape a question-and-answer session between guest and hosts. (Remember to inform mothers well in advance that they will be interviewed on tape.)

To ensure that children gather useful information, have them prepare questions to ask the mothers about their occupations and the ways in which these jobs changed their lifestyles. Questions might include the following: Where do you work? What is your job title? What kinds of tasks do you do? Describe the atmosphere of your workplace. What kind of training or education do you need for your job? Is it difficult to work both inside and outside the home? What do you like best about your work? What do you like least?

Provide class time for students to view excerpts from these videos, selected by small groups, if possible. Review the information briefly, then lead children through a **list/group/label** activity exploring the concept of the **working mom**. Allow children to share new understandings they have gained about the role of the working mother and its impact on family life.

Students can conclude this activity by photographing each working mother with her child or children who attend your school. Delegate small groups to mount each photo on posterboard, write a short caption describing the working mom, and present this keepsake in appreciation for her time and effort helping children learn.

ACTIVITY 3. This activity asks children to **consider their responsibilities at home in terms of gender roles and their impact on the quality of family life.** Set the stage for the activity by reading *Justin and the Best Biscuits in the World, Daddy Makes the Best Spaghetti, The Terrible Thing That Happened at Our House, The Long Red Scarf,* or all of these. Allow children to compare and contrast their chores and duties with those demonstrated in the stories. Help children draw conclusions about whether or not jobs seem gender specific (i.e., do only boys take out the trash?) and how they contribute to family welfare.

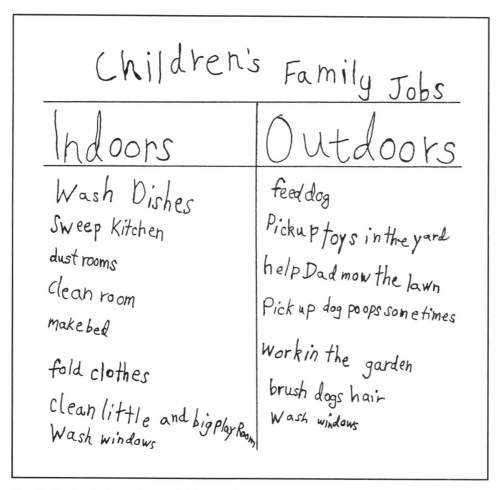

Fig. 5. A chart classifying children's family jobs. (*Maria Macia, age 8, Graciela Macia, age 6*)

To extend the activity, have small groups of students **categorize their family jobs**. On large sheets of butcher paper, groups might classify jobs by the degree of their impact on family life or whether they are performed indoors or outdoors. Culminate the activity by analyzing these charts in a whole-class discussion.

ACTIVITY 4. Several chapter 6 titles encourage children to **compare and contrast family roles and attitudes "then" and "now."** For example, *The Man Who Kept House; No, Agatha;* and *Roses Sing on New Snow: A Delicious Tale* provide glimpses of families past. After reading appropriate titles, help children find lifestyle examples to compare and contrast with their own experiences. Children might draw "then and now" pictures to illustrate their observations.

To extend the activity, class members might talk to grandparents about their responsibilities growing up, compared with children's duties today. After their conversations, children can share these amazing differences with classmates.

Activities of the Hand: Building Citizenship Skills

ACTIVITY 1. This activity helps children **create a timeline** showing the flow of significant events over their lifetimes. First, as you read selections aloud, highlight major changes that characters face, such as a new job (*The Terrible Thing That Happened at Our House*) or an illness (*Mr. Nick's Knitting*). Encourage children to talk with parents about equally important happenings in their own lives, such as the birth of a sibling, a move to a new home, or the loss of a grandparent. Review the basics of timeline building, then have students locate these significant events along a timeline drawn on a large sheet of construction paper. Have them caption these happenings and draw pictures that sketch their own life stories. In a large group discussion, establish similarities and differences among timelines.

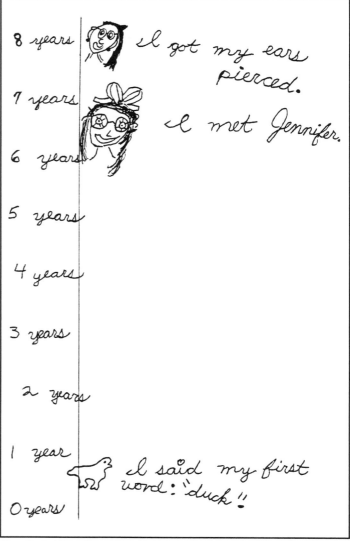

Fig. 6. A time-line showing events in a child's life. *(Rachel Korte, age 9)*

ACTIVITY 2. In this activity, students **practice some creative problem-solving and basic mapping skills** as they consider the special environments that many jobs require. Ask students to consider certain tasks in terms of space, time, and material needs. For example, an artist needs a brightly lit and well-equipped studio; a secretary needs a well-organized office with a desk and file space; and a farmer places livestock pens near shelter, food, and water sources. Once job requirements are understood, have children select an occupation and map an appropriate office, room, or work area on construction paper. When plans are finished, group children who chose similar occupations and allow them to compare their designs.

ACTIVITY 3. Many chapter titles are set in unusual places (e.g., *Katie Morag* on an island off the coast of Scotland). These stories offer opportunities for second- or third-graders to **develop geographic skills** as they become "geographic detectives." Assign a story with an unfamiliar setting to a pair or trio of students and ask them to uncover clues, such as architectural styles, weather patterns, landforms, and altitude, that pinpoint where the story takes place. Some settings will seem obvious; for others, ask probing questions to guide young detectives. After teams determine story locations, they can find them on a map. To conclude, review children's thought processes, paying particular attention to factors that made investigative techniques and geographic clues the most informative.

Activities of the Heart: Building Citizenship Dispositions

ACTIVITY 1. To **encourage children's appreciation for diverse family groups**, discuss how different families can be. Examine the kinds of people who make up a family, the roles of working members, and the kinds of dwellings in which families live. To inform children's dialogue, read aloud *Three Strong Women*, as the story provides an interesting look at a non-Western family situation. Other titles portray equally nontraditional families.

As the discussion winds down, create a class mural that includes a representation of each student's family group. Children can draw their families or make a collage. As enrichment, children might retell family stories that can be transcribed and compiled in a class anthology.

ACTIVITY 2. To help students **appreciate life from someone else's perspective**, arrange a job trade in which students and teacher switch roles. *Bea and Mr. Jones* and *The Man Who Kept House* provide humorous, yet revealing glimpses of the consequences of job trading. Individual students or small groups might plan and teach simple lessons. They might also complete the paperwork that accompanies most teaching tasks or attend a short faculty meeting or both. Encourage job traders to record their feelings and attitudes in a journal. Be sure to debrief all participants about their feelings and concerns as they looked at the world from someone else's viewpoint.

Section 3

Diversity in Terms of Physical Ability— Challenge or Handicap?

To promote civic competence, teachers and librarians should include **physical ability** among the categories of diversity that young citizens examine. Children must appreciate physically disabled people as well as individuals with mental disabilities or auditory or visual impairments. Through carefully chosen literature, educators can help children recognize that people with physical disabilities can achieve amazing things even though their bodies sometimes work only with great difficulty (chapter 7). They can show students that those with mental disabilities can live relatively full and rewarding lives (chapter 8). Educators can introduce the understanding that people with visual or auditory impairments often use other senses to "see" and to "hear" (chapter 9). Ultimately, children can judge whether physical disabilities seem impossible handicaps that prohibit the practice of citizenship or daunting challenges that can be overcome. Students can also gain the knowledge, interpersonal skills, and empathy that increase their civic competence.

Chapter 7

Physical Disabilities—Only My Body Doesn't Work Well!

This chapter advances the argument that physically disabled people can marshal inner resources to accomplish amazing things. Children need to appreciate that people who have disabled bodies can be enabled in many important ways. The literature chosen for this chapter can help teachers and librarians introduce students to the incredible range of human abilities that they will encounter every day as citizens. We feature *The Balancing Girl* because it presents people with physical disabilities in an upbeat yet realistic manner. Alternate and related titles offer additional support for the chapter theme and provide options for teaching about the ways people respond to disability.

Feature Title

The Balancing Girl by Berniece Rabe. Illus. by Lillian Hoban. New York: Dutton Children's Books, 1981. 32p. ISBN 0-525-26160-5.

Margaret, who wears full-leg braces and often uses a wheelchair, is still the best balancer in her first-grade class. Bright and capable, she proposes an idea, then works hard to translate her plan into the most successful booth at the school carnival.

As they visit Margaret's classroom, children can see social studies dispositions, such as empathy, responsibility, and respect for human dignity, demonstrated in a familiar setting. Additionally, Rabe's story clearly introduces learning experiences that promote social interaction, conflict resolution, and problem solving.

Alternate Titles

Harry and Willy and Carrothead by Judith Caseley. New York: Greenwillow Books, 1991. 24p. ISBN 0-688-09493-7.

Harry is a confident kindergartner who can easily manipulate the prosthesis that has replaced his left arm. Besides his physical dexterity, Harry can reassure his classmates that everything is okay with a kind word and an engaging smile.

Caseley's story relates important citizenship understandings in terms that children can understand. First, physical disabilities do not always equal personal and social problems. Second, emphasizing similarities is often more productive than noting differences. And third, no citizen can prosper without a healthy supply of self-respect.

Nick Joins In by Joe Lasker. Morton Grove, IL: A. Whitman, 1980. 32p. ISBN 0-807-55612-2.

A wheelchair user, Nick has grown accustomed to classmates and teachers coming to him. Still, Nick adjusts well to his new school by doing what he can and downplaying what he cannot do.

Lasker's story invites civic dialogue and conversation. Children can grasp the citizenship implications of this excellent read-aloud title as they compare and contrast Nick's situation with their own. Teachers can also engage students in the many skill-building exercises that the story suggests, such as problem solving, social interaction, and information gathering.

Ride the Red Cycle by Harriette Robinet. Illus. by David Brown. Boston: Houghton Mifflin, 1980. 34p. ISBN 0-395-29183-6.

Eleven-year-old Jerome, disabled by a disease for nine years, often gets angry at being so dependent on others. Struggling to increase his independence, Jerome learns to ride a tricycle, then displays his new abilities at a neighborhood gathering.

Although this is an older, somewhat didactic story, the book offers young readers some valuable citizenship lessons. Children can watch Jerome recognize a problem, take the initiative, and resolve the difficulty. As he takes action, Jerome develops his self-concept and increases his physical skills as well as his ability to relate to others.

Related Titles

Anna Joins In by Katrin Arnold. Illus. by Renate Seelig. Nashville, TN: Abingdon Press, 1983. 32p. ISBN 0-687-01530-8.

Anna, a kindergartner who has cystic fibrosis, must deal constantly with the physical problems of her disease as well as its social and emotional consequences.

A Contest by Sherry N. Payne. Illus. by Jeff Kyle. Minneapolis, MN: Carolrhoda Books, 1982. 37p. ISBN 0-876-14176-9.

After being in a special school for several years, Mike, who has cerebral palsy, enters a fifth-grade classroom in a public school. With his teacher's encouragement, Mike and his classmates better appreciate his inner strengths as well as his obvious needs.

Darlene by Eloise Greenfield. Illus. by George Ford. New York: Methuen, 1980. 32p. ISBN 0-416-30701-9.

At first, Darlene does not want to visit her uncle and cousin; she only wants to go home. However, Darlene's wheelchair doesn't stop her cousin from playing games with her. By the time her mother returns, Darlene no longer wants to leave; she is having too much fun!

Grandma Drives a Motor Bed by Diane J. Hamm. Illus. by Charles Robinson. Morton Grove, IL: A. Whitman, 1987. 32p. ISBN 0-807-53025-5.

Hamm invites young readers to observe as family and friends deal with Grandma's paralysis. Though the pictures are not the best, the story offers positive role models for social interaction and personal problem solving.

Grandma's Wheelchair by Lorraine Henriod. Illus. by Christa Chevalier. Morton Grove, IL: A. Whitman, 1982. ISBN 0-807-53035-2.

Four-year-old Thomas spends weekday mornings with his grandmother, who uses a wheelchair. Together, they accomplish many things and provide young citizens with new insights about overcoming physical disability.

The Potato Man by Megan McDonald. Illus. by Ted Lewin. New York: Orchard, 1991. 32p. ISBN 0-531-08514-7.

Grandpa tells his grandchildren about boyhood encounters with a one-eyed vegetable peddler. Initially terrified, Grandpa learned to see beyond the Potato Man's disability and welcome his kindness.

Princess Pooh by Kathleen M. Muldoon. Illus. by Linda Shute. Morton Grove, IL: A. Whitman, 1989. 32p. ISBN 0-807-56627-6.

Patty is jealous of the extra attention given her older sister, Penelope. After she rides in Penelope's wheelchair, Patty's jealousy fades as she begins to understand her sister's condition.

Teaching Options

After reading *The Balancing Girl* or any of the alternate and related titles, introduce one or more of the following activities. Most are not designed for specific titles but may work better with some books than with others. We hope you will consider modifying these ideas to fit your teaching situation and incorporating multiple books into a particular activity.

Activities of the Head: Building Citizenship Understandings

ACTIVITY 1. After reading *The Balancing Girl*, *Nick Joins In*, *Harry and Willy and Carrothead*, *Princess Pooh*, or *Grandma Drives a Motor Bed*, try this activity **to expand children's knowledge of the many devices that afford mobility to people with physical disabilities:** wheelchairs, canes, walkers, crutches, and prostheses. Many children may not know anyone who relies on an appliance to get around, so bring sample devices into the classroom for children to try. Because it is very important that students approach these appliances seriously and use them properly, invite guest speakers to talk with the class about their use. Pair children and let them tackle classroom routines using particular devices (e.g., writing on the chalkboard; working at a desk or computer; going to the playground). In a large group setting, encourage pairs to compare and contrast their experiences with the ways in which they normally complete these tasks. Conclude by asking each student to illustrate her or his new understandings. If possible, appoint a student committee to share these drawings with the guest speakers.

ACTIVITY 2. As they analyze their school's floor plan, students **better understand the need to make public buildings accessible to people using appliances**. Revisit the titles featured in activity 1, particularly those with school settings. As you discuss these stories, ask children to cite instances where the characters have trouble navigating around the building and grounds. Group children in trios and have them record these potential trouble spots for future reference. Armed with this information, allow trios to tour their campus, predicting potential problem areas. To determine accessibility, provide groups with tape measures and yardsticks as well as the approximate sizes of common appliances. If a judgment call arises, encourage children to consult an outside expert, such as a knowledgeable parent or a classmate on crutches. Recruit older students and parents to help children lacking measurement or computational skills.

Ph.4. Trio surveying potential trouble area. *(Arna Zwicher, Kaleena Hoyne, Chris Kesner)*

As trios report their findings to the class, ask them to indicate whether there are "inches to spare" or "inches needed." On a simple map of the school, shade areas that are readily accessible in green; mark problem areas in yellow or red. Have students analyze the map to assess whether or not they could participate in school events if they relied on an appliance for mobility. To empower young citizens, inform them that the *Federal Americans with Disabilities Act* guarantees open access to physically disabled people. Allow them to bring problem areas to the principal's attention.

ACTIVITY 3. This activity helps students **understand that appliances are labor-saving devices for persons with physical disabilities. Although the devices can frustrate at times, they make life much easier overall.** After reading one or more titles aloud, brainstorm labor-saving devices that most people rely on every day, such as microwave ovens, washing machines, and lawn mowers. Compare and contrast them with appliances for people who are physically disabled. If necessary, help children differentiate between labor-saving devices and communication devices (e.g., radios, TVs, VCRs) so that children focus on things that save time and effort rather than things that entertain. Ask students to describe appliances in terms of what they accomplish, why they were created, and whom they were meant to assist.

To extend the activity, small groups of older primary students might research who invented particular appliances, when they were developed, and where they were first used. Student groups might also survey members of the school community to assess how many have used selected devices such as crutches and wheelchairs and what benefits they received.

ACTIVITY 4. To expand students' awareness of the special needs of people with physical disabilities, arrange for them to explore a school bus or van equipped for children who use wheelchairs. Introduce this activity by reading aloud selected stories in which main characters travel to school on a special vehicle. *Nick Joins In* is a good choice, because Nick rides a small yellow bus. Then children can compile a list of questions to ask after the driver describes the equipment and demonstrates how it works. When children return to the classroom, allow them to record what they have learned in their journals and discuss their new knowledge with classmates.

ACTIVITY 5. This activity reinforces the notion that **specially trained animals as well as mechanical devices assist persons with physical disabilities in accomplishing daily tasks**. Allow children to rotate through a series of multimedia centers acquainting them with animal helpers in action. For example, construct a photo and trade book display demonstrating the many ways that animals serve people with physical disabilities. Or create a video station showing how these animals are trained. Before exiting the rotation, children should visit a writing center and record three ways that animals help people with special needs. Provide class time for children to share these observations.

Activities of the Hand: Building Citizenship Skills

ACTIVITY 1. This experience incorporates understandings from *Nick Joins In* and *A Contest* with information gained in previous activities to **promote children's problem-solving and map skills**. After reading the stories, remind students that the main characters enter public schools after learning in specialized environments, one at home and the other in a school. Help children recognize that, like Nick and Mike, most people must adapt to changing circumstances. Then review the knowledge gained in Head activities 1 and 2 about appliances and how they help people adapt to difficult surroundings. Group children and assign each team an area in the school that might present barriers to people with physical disabilities. Have each group map the problem area, then prepare a second map illustrating renovations that might make the area more accessible. Let groups share their before and after maps with classmates and building administrators.

ACTIVITY 2. Several titles introduce opportunities for children to **build creative problem-solving skills.** In *Harry and Willy and Carrothead*, for example, a prosthesis has replaced Harry's left arm, somewhat limiting his dexterity. In *Ride the Red Cycle*, Jerome cannot ride a tricycle until his father modifies the bike to meet his needs. Read these stories aloud and discuss how these clever devices help young people overcome handicaps.

This is for someone who wants to have fun even if one leg is shorter than the other.

← piece of wood

Fig. 7. Design for gadget/appliance. *(Rachel Korte, age 9)*

Then challenge students to invent a gadget to solve an everyday problem that a physically disabled person might face. Encourage children to construct a model of their invention from "trash treasures" like cardboard tubes, straws, clay, old buttons, rubber bands, toothpicks, and pipe cleaners. So users can maximize benefits, remind children to write instructions for the gadget or dictate them to an older student or parent helper. If time permits, children can showcase their inventions for classmates and invited guests.

Activities of the Heart: Building Citizenship Dispositions

ACTIVITY 1. Characters in this chapter's stories overcome physical impairments to achieve personal goals, but struggle mightily as they do so. **To help students better understand such frustrations,** find ways to limit them temporarily as they tackle routine tasks. For example, children might wear bulky mittens while picking up a penny, walk with their ankles hobbled, or wear a blindfold while delivering something across the room. To debrief the activity, pair children and ask them to relate their experiences to one another, particularly the feelings generated by their unfamiliar clumsiness and classmates' reactions to their awkwardness. Then convene a large group session and let volunteers relate their feelings. As the sharing proceeds, prompt suggestions about the best ways to react when encountering a person who must struggle to meet physical challenges.

ACTIVITY 2. This activity encourages children to ponder **how people different from each other on the outside are often similar on the inside**. In a large group discussion, encourage students to contrast physical traits that seem very different (e.g., hair color, weight, height). Then pair students who seem to be opposites and let them role-play a chance meeting in which they discover common interests, backgrounds, opinions, and attitudes. Follow by reading aloud *The Potato Man*. In a class conversation about the story, guide children to the observation that the peddler seemed dramatically different from the children (e.g., he had one eye; he was much older; his manner was gruff), but he shared a common kindness and sensitivity. Encourage children to conclude that physical differences seem quite insignificant compared to the inner qualities that people share.

ACTIVITY 3. To promote empathy and understanding, read several of the preceding storybooks and ask children to put themselves in the shoes of physically disabled characters. Arrange for selected students to visit with physically disabled people and share their reactions with classmates. If possible, invite a guest speaker with a disability to dialogue with the class. Appoint a student committee to moderate the conversation; help members prepare questions that foster an open exchange of feelings and ideas. For example, students might ask about mechanical and mobility issues, about the emotional costs of confronting a sometimes hostile environment, and about safety concerns. They might ask the visitor how people react to him or her and how she or he would prefer them to react. Although the committee should determine the interview, ensure time for discussion, demonstration of any appliances that the speaker may use, and questions from the floor.

Chapter 8

Understanding Mental Disabilities— Sometimes My Brain Fails Me

This chapter emphasizes the theme that persons with mental disabilities can practice citizenship in fuller and more rewarding ways than stereotypes often suggest. Admittedly, age-appropriate stories featuring characters with brain damage and other mental disabilities seem relatively few in number. Still, our booklist demonstrates that interested teachers and librarians can track down relevant, quality literature to share with young children. The featured title, *Making Room for Uncle Joe*, elaborates how a Down's syndrome adult and his relatives adjust to life together after he moves into their home. Additional titles expand opportunities for primary children to gain insights regarding people with mental disabilities as well as the knowledge, skills, and dispositions to practice informed social decision making.

Feature Title

Making Room for Uncle Joe by Ada Bassett Litchfield. Illus. by Gail Owens. Morton Grove, IL: A. Whitman, 1984. 30p. ISBN 0-807-54952-5.

> Three children make adjustments and experience frustrations when Uncle Joe comes to visit for a while. Because he has Down's syndrome, Uncle Joe sometimes thinks and acts in ways that seem strange. However, as family members adapt, they agree to make Uncle Joe's visit a permanent arrangement and express joy that he will stay "all the time, forever."

This story introduces many opportunities to acquire and apply social-studies competencies such as communicating ideas and following directions. Additionally, children can meet Uncle Joe, spend time with his family, and gain knowledge about Down's syndrome. With these understandings, children can forge a bond with Uncle Joe and recognize stereotypical treatment of people with mental handicaps. Although acceptance of Uncle Joe's behavior might not come easily, students should at least agree that a caring family can reconcile attitudes toward his disability and deal constructively with his condition.

Alternate Titles

My Sister's Special by Jo Prall. Photos by Linda Gray. Chicago: Children's Press, 1985. 31p. ISBN 0-516-03862-1.

> When Angie was very young, her brain was deprived of oxygen during a serious illness, leaving Angie unable to talk or use her arms and legs like other family

members. Because they love her so much, her brothers focus on Angie's many strengths rather than her physical and mental handicaps.

This sensitive story introduces young readers to a peer who regularly takes civic action despite many serious disabilities. As she communicates her thoughts with a language board or participates in school functions, Angie regularly models the Head, Hand, and Heart of citizenship in ways that primary children can acknowledge and emulate.

Sachiko Means Happiness by Kimiko Sakai. Illus. by Tomie Arai. San Francisco: Children's Book Press, 1990. 32p. ISBN 0-892-39065-4.

Grandmother no longer recognizes Sachiko because advancing Alzheimer's disease hampers her memory. Initially upset by her loved one's forgetfulness, Sachiko soon realizes that some creative problem solving can enable her and Grandmother to enjoy their time together.

Sakai's picture book explores a disease that causes many people to make painful decisions affecting friends and family members. Sachiko's story encourages students to understand this condition better and empathize with its many victims. In time, children might take civic action that would improve the quality of life for both young and old.

Related Titles

Always Gramma by Vaunda Micheaux Nelson. Illus. by Kimanne Uhler. New York: Putnam, 1988. 32p. ISBN 0-399-21542-5.

A girl is confused, distressed, and sad when Gramma gets so mixed up from what appears to be Alzheimer's disease that she requires 24-hour care in a nursing home. Fortunately, her granddaughter can visit frequently and cheer Gramma with familiar stories.

Don't Look at Me: A Child's Book About Feeling Different by Doris Sanford. Illus. by Graci Evans. Portland, OR: Multnomah Press, 1986. 27p. ISBN 0-880-70150-1.

In school, Patrick seems slow and does not like himself much. He listens to his talking lamb friend, Fluffy, who suggests that he address one problem at a time. One evening, Patrick and his grandpa study spelling words and then set Patrick's next goal—getting along better with classmates.

Grandpa Doesn't Know It's Me by Donna Guthrie. Illus. by Katy Keck Arnsteen. New York: Human Sciences Press, 1986. 29p. ISBN 0-898-85302-8.

Grandpa has always visited Elizabeth and her family, but he comes to live with them full-time when Alzheimer's disease causes his health to fail. Though Grandpa rarely recognizes her, Elizabeth still spends time with him, developing insights about his disease that she shares with young readers.

Uncle Melvin by Daniel Pinkwater. New York: Macmillan, 1989. 32p. ISBN 0-027-74675-5.

Every morning, Uncle Melvin leaves the "looney bin," as he calls it, to work around the house and garden with his nephew. When Charles asks about his uncle's odd comments, his father observes, "Melvin sees the world in his own way." Through Uncle Melvin's example, children realize that family love and proper care can help an emotionally disturbed person regain social and personal competence.

Where's Chimpy? by Berniece Rabe. Photos by Diane Schmidt. Morton Grove, IL: A. Whitman, 1988. 32p. ISBN 0-807-58928-4.

Misty's stuffed monkey, Chimpy, should go to sleep, but he turns up missing. She and her dad finally track him down and get him ready for bed. The story helps young children recognize that they share many needs, wants, and abilities with Misty, a Down's syndrome child.

Wilfrid Gordon McDonald Partridge by Mem Fox. Illus. by Julie Vivas. New York: Kane/Miller, 1985. 32p. ISBN 0-916-29104-9.

Wilfrid's good friends live in a home for the elderly near his house. After overhearing his parents remark that Miss Nancy has lost her memory, he sets out to help her find it. By gathering memories for Miss Nancy, he revives her past and restores her dignity.

Teaching Options

The following activities can be introduced after reading *Making Room for Uncle Joe* or any other titles listed for this chapter. Although most activities do not depend on a specific book, they may be better suited to some books than others. These teaching ideas should be adjusted to fit your classroom needs. Allow children to compare and contrast ideas by including multiple stories in particular activities. As you implement any of these activities, remember that mental disability can be an extremely personal and sensitive topic. Encourage students to connect chapter stories with personal experiences and to participate in class conversations but avoid forcing their involvement.

Activities of the Head: Building Citizenship Understandings

ACTIVITY 1. After reading *Making Room for Uncle Joe* or other relevant titles, help primary children expand their **understanding of mental handicaps by comparing and contrasting myths versus truths**. In a large group discussion, carefully examine characters' misconceptions about the consequences of Uncle Joe's appearance and behavior. For example, because he has a squashed-in nose, is unusual looking, and drools constantly, his young relatives are convinced that they will never have friends over. Then pair students and charge them with collecting other people's perceptions of persons with mental disabilities. Children might consult classmates, school faculty, community members, and family members. Before interviewing begins, help students generate appropriate questions to guide data gathering.

As students report their findings, chart responses in two columns, one labeled "Myths," and the other "Truths." Older students can assign information into the appropriate columns. Help younger children determine where particular ideas should be placed. To wrap up the activity, invite a guest expert to assist students as they separate myths from truths, dispel false information, and produce meaningful conclusions.

ACTIVITY 2. This straightforward activity yields **considerable understanding about symptoms that accompany mentally handicapping conditions.** After reading particular titles, ask the media specialist, knowledgeable colleagues, social service professionals, or all three to help small groups pursue reliable information about disabling illnesses or injuries or both. Each group should record two or three factual statements about a handicapping condition, including Down's syndrome (after reading *Making Room for Uncle Joe* and *Where's Chimpy?*), oxygen deprivation (*My Sister's Special*), dementia (*Wilfrid Gordon McDonald Partridge*), and Alzheimer's disease (*Sachiko Means Happiness*, *Always Gramma*, *Grandpa Doesn't Know It's Me*). Provide children with time to share information with the rest of the class and dialogue about its implications.

ACTIVITY 3. Read aloud *My Sister's Special*, then spark children's **knowledge of the functions of a unique and important organ, the human brain**. Use models and other visuals to help students locate areas of the brain that might control routine behaviors. Is one part of the brain in charge of walking? Which area controls talking? What happens when a section of the brain is injured or diseased and cannot work properly? Invite a local expert, such as the school psychologist or a physician, to answer questions about the ways in which the brain operates and how these functions distinguish human beings from other living things. Children should discover that the brain allows us to accomplish an infinite number of thoughts and actions. Help them realize that a person can still manage amazing mental and physical feats even though his or her brain cannot function at peak efficiency.

To conclude, brainstorm tasks, behaviors, and subject areas that children tackle every day in school, such as math, writing, singing, kicking a soccer ball, sharpening a pencil, comparing shapes, and identifying colors. List as many large and small accomplishments as possible on a sheet of butcher paper. Then let children dialogue in small groups about the brain's central role in performing these activities. Encourage the conclusion that the human mind requires extraordinary sophistication to complete even the simplest task. Allow children to illustrate the list and post it as a bulletin board. As the year progresses, children can add items and revisit the issue of the brain's uniqueness and importance.

Activities of the Hand: Building Citizenship Skills

ACTIVITY 1. After students have considered this chapter's stories and studied mental disabilities, they should appreciate that people have inherent value and dignity, regardless of their functional ability. So children can **apply this understanding and polish their communication skills,** establish a regular connection with members of a sheltered workshop for the developmentally disabled. To provide background information, reread *Making Room for Uncle Joe* and remind children that Joe will work at a sheltered workshop. Students can send class-made cards, drawings, letters, and pictures to introduce themselves and encourage a regular exchange with the clients.

Dear Joe,
   My name is Joshua. I am nine years old. I will send you a picture of my self the next time I write. In my spare time I like to play with legos.
   What do you do at the sheltered workshop, and in your spare time?
                           your friend,
                           Joshua
   P.S. send me a picture of your self.

Fig. 8. Sample correspondence to a workshop client. *(Joshua Betts, age 9)*

To extend the activity, motivate children to become active citizens, researching community services for people with special needs and disseminating this information to interested community members. Students might even publicize these services in school newsletters, or contact media representatives to place news accounts on television or in the newspaper, or both.

ACTIVITY 2. This experience provides an opportunity for children **to formulate and give directions for a simple problem-solving task**. After reading *Don't Look at Me*, or *Where's Chimpy?*, or both, guide children to the observation that not everyone understands directions at the same rate or in the same way. To reinforce this conclusion, ask students to give complete directions for a simple task such as folding a shirt, opening a bottle, or making a sandwich. Allow time for students to record a logical set of directions, with assistance if necessary, then pair each young teacher with an older student learner. Instruct the learners to follow the directions exactly as written. After the task is completed, have partners talk about the difficulties that they encountered and possible ways to improve the effectiveness and clarity of the directions. After the older students return to their classroom, bring children together in a large group session. Ask them to consider why most people need detailed instructions to comprehend and complete a task, and speculate why some people need even more specific directions and more time to digest them than others.

Activities of the Heart: Building Citizenship Dispositions

ACTIVITY 1. Many children might not realize that people who have severe mental or physical handicaps often reside in nursing homes or other long-term care facilities. **To help students appreciate the nature of long-term care and empathize with the situations demanding it,** invite a staff member from a local facility to interact with the class. Before the speaker visits, familiarize children with the notion of long-term care by reading pertinent stories aloud. For example, Wilfrid's friend, Miss Nancy, resides in a nursing home near his house (*Wilfrid Gordon McDonald Partridge*). Charles's uncle lives in a care facility that he humorously labels the "looney bin" (*Uncle Melvin*).

To extend this activity, older primary children could learn "Let There Be Peace on Earth," or other suitable songs or poems about getting along with all kinds of people. Then they could visit a nursing home, preferably the one where the guest speaker works, to perform the song and talk in small groups with the "grandmas" and "grandpas" who live there. If children are unfamiliar with care facilities, take pre-visit class time to brief them about the unusual and sometimes unsettling sights, sounds, and smells there. Follow the field trip with opportunities for children to reflect on their experiences, in journals if possible, and share their thoughts and feelings with classmates.

ACTIVITY 2. Sometimes persons with mental disabilities are termed "special people," as in the stories *My Sister's Special* and *Don't Look at Me*. In fact, most schools have special education programs for children who learn with some difficulty. **Promote understanding of and positive attitudes toward special people** through ongoing class conversations about the word *special*. Read aloud selected picture books to generate these discussions. As dialogue continues, lead children to the conclusion that everyone is special in some way. For one thing, all citizens have special obligations to meet and tasks to perform, regardless of their intellectual capacities, such as doing their best work, listening well, and respecting others. Brainstorm a list of duties that every young citizen should fulfill and discuss ways in which special people might address these responsibilities. Conclude by asking children to role-play these suggestions in small groups.

ACTIVITY 3. This activity **confirms the universal truth that everyone perceives the world from her or his point of view.** Read aloud several books that examine a particular mental handicap from different perspectives. As older primary children talk about these stories, encourage them to give reasons why a character displayed a particular mind-set. If reading abilities permit, have them support their ideas with specific quotations. As the conversation proceeds, guide students to the observation that different points of view should not be judged in terms of right versus wrong or good versus bad. Many factors shade the perspectives that people take and explain why they were taken. These factors range from cultural background, experiential level, and language differences to lack of information and reliance on input from a questionable source.

To extend the activity, stage an incident in the classroom that children might interpret in different ways. Debrief the dramatization thoroughly, first by asking each child to compare his or her assessment of the situation with a partner's, then by allowing students to share their conclusions about point of view in a large group setting.

ACTIVITY 4. To build awareness of stereotyping and the damage that thoughtless comments can cause, hold class meetings in which children clarify the meanings of labels often attached carelessly to people who appear different in some way. Begin dialogue with a meaningful passage from a picture book. In *Don't Look at Me*, for example, a classmate calls Patrick several derogatory names, including "stupid" and "old retard." Let children brainstorm other words often hurled at people who appear less than capable. Talk about the curious ways in which these words can have little explicit meaning but great capacity for hurting feelings and damaging self-esteem. Encourage children to talk about situations in which they might encounter people who are different (school, church, grocery). After suggesting a situation, have them role-play the encounter without labeling anyone except by using their names. Then have students discuss the encounter with an outsider (a third party) and model statements like, "Joe, who needs my help to count his change."

Chapter 9

Visual and Auditory Impairments—
Adapting Other Senses
to See and Hear

Section 3's final chapter communicates the message that citizens with visual or auditory impairments can compensate for missing faculties to an amazing degree. These individuals often magnify their other senses, adapting other forms of sensory input to "see" and "hear" their world. As they make social decisions, people with visual or auditory impairments may also use aids and appliances to gather information and dialogue with others. Throughout this chapter's recommended literature, characters model important understandings, skills, and values that young citizens can recognize and perhaps emulate. We feature *Through Grandpa's Eyes* because reviewers and young readers have repeatedly cited the book's sensitive tone and lasting message. The alternate and related titles further emphasize the chapter theme and increase opportunities to promote children's civic competence.

Feature Title

Through Grandpa's Eyes by Patricia MacLachlan. Illus. by Deborah Ray. New York: HarperCollins, 1979. 48p. ISBN 0-060-22560-2.

A boy wonders how Grandpa can do so many things so well despite his blindness. As John spends time visiting his grandparents, he discovers that his grandfather employs a keen sense of touch to maneuver indoors and acute listening skills to enjoy the outdoors more fully. Preparing to return home, John has become so sensitized that he can close his eyes and "hear" the smile on his grandmother's face. For the first time, John perceives the world "through Grandpa's eyes."

By affording children glimpses of a blind person leading an active life, MacLachlan helps them better appreciate citizens with disabilities. Young people might also sense the positive energy that supportive, caring family members can offer. Finally, the story accurately portrays the ways in which a handicapped person explores and makes meaning from his physical and social environments.

Alternate Titles

Buffy's Orange Leash by Stephen Golder and Lise Memling. Illus. by Marcy Ramsey. Washington, DC: Kendall Green Publications, 1988. 32p. ISBN 0-930-32342-4.

Buffy's orange leash advertises his status as a helper dog. Because his owners are deaf, Buffy serves the Johnsons as a hearing dog, alerting them to such noises as telephone calls, smoke alarms, and a crying baby. The book walks young readers through Buffy's selection process and training regimen, as well as the daily tasks that he enables his owners to perform with relative ease.

Like MacLachlan, Golder and Memling promote children's understanding of the extent to which sensory-impaired people can exercise the rights and responsibilities of citizenship. Their story nurtures empathy for the Johnsons, a deaf couple with a young child, and encourages respect for the ways in which they manage a demanding schedule with the assistance of a hearing dog. The book might also introduce problem-solving and decision-making experiences for primary students.

Happy Birthday, Grampie by Susan Pearson. Illus. by Ronald Himler. New York: Dial Books for Young Readers, 1987. 32p. ISBN 0-803-73458-1.

Young Martha travels with her family to visit her beloved Grampie, who happens to be blind. She thinks long and hard to identify a birthday gift that her grandfather will remember always. Martha creates a personalized birthday card with a heart made of felt and stick-on letters that Grampie can "read" with his fingers.

Pearson's book increases children's understanding of the ways in which blind citizens cope with their special circumstances. Students also encounter a primary-age girl modeling reflective thinking and creative problem-solving skills. Additionally, children might broaden their appreciation of physical diversity and gain empathy as they witness Martha and her grandfather sharing a special moment.

A Very Special Friend by Dorothy Hoffman Levi. Illus. by Ethel Gold. Washington, DC: Kendall Green Publications, 1989. 40p. ISBN 0-930-32355-6.

When a new girl moves into the neighborhood, six-year-old Frannie desperately wants to be friends. To her surprise and frustration, Frannie discovers that she cannot talk with Laura because she is deaf. After a few false starts, the two new friends overcome communication differences and enjoy playing together.

Levi packs this title with potential citizenship lessons. After reading and considering the story, primary students might better distinguish people's differences and similarities; they might make and keep friends more easily; they might get along more productively in the classroom. Finally, they might communicate more fluently using alternative modes of expression like sign language and finger spelling, and solve personal problems more effectively.

Related Titles

Amy, the Story of a Deaf Child by Lou Ann Walker. Photos by Michael Abramson. New York: Lodestar, 1985. 60p. ISBN 0-525-67145-5.

The photos and text in this nonfiction book chronicle a day in the life of a deaf fifth-grader. Amy uses hearing aids and sign language to attend a regular school and participate in normal activities.

A Cane in Her Hand by Ada Bassett Litchfield. Illus. by Eleanor Mill. Morton Grove, IL: A. Whitman, 1977. 32p. ISBN 0-807-51056-4.

In a frank conversation with young readers, a girl reveals that her impaired vision may lead to total blindness and explains the many frustrations she faces. She also describes the help she has received from family, friends, medical personnel, and school staff members.

The Day We Met Cindy by Anne M. Starowitz. Illus. by first-grade students. Washington, DC: Gallaudet, 1988. 16p. ISBN 0-930-32343-2.

After meeting a classmate's deaf aunt, a group of first-graders learn sign language so they can share Christmas songs with the girl's family. The book's caring tone and very personal illustrations by first-graders make it distinctive and meaningful.

The Gift by Helen Coutant. Illus. by Vo-Dinh Mai. New York: Alfred A. Knopf, 1983. 45p. ISBN 0-394-95499-8.

Anna gives Nana Marie, an older friend who has become blind, a delightful, intangible gift—the solemn promise to visit regularly and recount the wonders that she encounters each day.

A Guide Dog Puppy Grows Up by Caroline Arnold. Photos by Richard Hewett. San Diego, CA: Harcourt Brace Jovanovich, 1991. 48p. ISBN 0-152-32657-X.

In this nonfiction title, a puppy completes training as a Seeing Eye dog, then serves as a guide for Anne Gelles, a blind teacher of blind children.

Handtalk Birthday by Remy Charlip and Mary B. Miller. Illus. by George Ancona. New York: Macmillan, 1987. 42p. ISBN 0-027-18080-8.

Charlip relates a traditional story—Mary Beth's friends throw her a surprise birthday party—in a nontraditional manner—through finger spelling and sign language.

I Have a Sister—My Sister Is Deaf by Jeanne Whitehouse Peterson. Illus. by Deborah Ray. New York: HarperCollins, 1977. 32p. ISBN 0-060-24702-9.

The narrator elaborates how her deaf sister turns potentially daunting challenges into everyday experiences by compensating in various ways, such as lip-reading, sensing sound vibrations, and tuning-in to body language.

My Favorite Place by Susan Sargent and Donna Aaron Wirt. Illus. by Allan Eitzen. Nashville, TN: Abingdon Press, 1983. 16p. ISBN 0-687-27538-5.

At the end of this appealing story about a family's day at the beach, the young narrator reveals for the first time that she is blind.

My Friend Leslie: The Story of a Handicapped Child by Maxine B. Rosenberg. Photos by George Ancona. New York: Lothrop, Lee & Shepard, 1983. 48p. ISBN 0-688-01691-X.

This nonfiction title follows Leslie as she tackles her daily routine—riding the school bus, painting a beautiful picture, making soup, reading a favorite story, and playing at recess—despite severe, multiple disabilities.

A Place for Grace by Jean Davies Okimoto. Illus. by Doug Keith. Seattle, WA: Sasquatch Books, 1993. 32p. ISBN 0-912-365-73-0.

In this humorous story, Okimoto chronicles a little dog's transformation from street dog to helper dog for a hearing-impaired man.

The Seal Oil Lamp adapted from an Eskimo folktale by Dale DeArmond. San Francisco: Sierra Club Books, 1988. 32p. ISBN 0-316-17786-5.

Older primary children should enjoy and discover many citizenship learnings from this Inuit legend. Kinfolk abandon a blind boy, because tribal law demands extreme action when someone's physical problems threaten group survival. But the Mouse People repay a past kindness by teaching the boy survival skills. After many trials, he becomes a hunter, accepted by his tribe.

See You Tomorrow, Charles by Miriam Cohen. Illus. by Lillian Hoban. New York: Greenwillow Books, 1983. 32p. ISBN 0-688-01804-1.

Charles and his first-grade classmates recognize his obvious limitations as he struggles with obstacles raised by his blindness. They also discover Charles's impressive strengths as he leads three classmates from a dark basement in which he alone can navigate.

Watch Out, Ronald Morgan! by Patricia Reilly Giff. Illus. by Susanna Natti. New York: Viking Kestrel, 1985. 32p. ISBN 0-670-80433-9.

Ronald's myopic astigmatism causes many humorous mishaps at school until he gets his first pair of glasses. He soon realizes that eyeglasses might lessen problems, but they do not solve them all!

Teaching Options

Any of this chapter's titles might spark any of the following activities that meet your students' needs and fit your classroom situation. As in past chapters, these teaching ideas are not tied to specific titles, can be modified as necessary, and might work even better when multiple stories are integrated. Finally, many children have some acquaintance with individuals who are visually or auditorily impaired. Yet they may still require careful explanation and caring guidance to move beyond superficial knowledge to attain deeper understanding.

Activities of the Head: Building Citizenship Understandings

ACTIVITY 1. To stimulate student inquiry about the senses, especially hearing and sight, read *Through Grandpa's Eyes, My Friend Leslie, A Cane in Her Hand, Watch Out, Ronald Morgan!,* or similar stories. Invite an ophthalmologist and an otolaryngologist to speak with the class. Perhaps the experts can bring replicas of the eye and ear to show students. After the doctors briefly discuss eye and ear functions, encourage students to examine the models and pose questions. Ask the guests to explain the most likely conditions or events that can cause blindness or deafness; encourage them to stress eye and ear safety as well as proper care for these vital sensory organs.

To conclude, pair students and have them illustrate the most important new knowledge that the guest speakers provided. If time permits, student pairs might create large posters showing situations where safety equipment would keep ears and eyes safe, such as batting helmets while playing baseball, goggles while using power tools, and ear plugs while swimming. Provide class time for partners to share their ideas and post their visuals around the school.

ACTIVITY 2. This learning experience allows children to **gain insights about the animal helpers that assist people who are visually impaired or hearing impaired**. Begin by reading aloud two titles that focus on guide dogs. *Buffy's Orange Leash* and the humorous story, *A Place for Grace*, enlighten children about hearing dogs, while the nonfiction title, *A Guide Dog Puppy Grows Up* deals with the selection and preparation of a Seeing Eye dog. As you share these titles, encourage students to compare and contrast the ways in which the animals help their owners function. To link the literature directly to real life, ask a person who has a hearing ear or Seeing Eye dog to demonstrate the contributions that the dog makes to his or her personal and social welfare.

Should children want additional information about these important animals, ask the librarian or media specialist to locate a film, videotape, or audiotape detailing the selection, training, and functions of guide dogs around the world. With assistance, children might also contact local experts and organizations that put blind and deaf persons in touch with the services of guide dogs. If time permits, create a forum in which young investigators can share new knowledge with classmates.

ACTIVITY 3. Provide opportunities to inspect visual and auditory aids like glasses, contact lenses, hearing aids, and headphones **so children can be informed about the relative advantages and disadvantages of ear and eye appliances**. To introduce the activity, read *Watch Out, Ronald Morgan!*, as the book furnishes a humorous look at the rewards and pitfalls of wearing eyeglasses. After briefly reviewing the story, group children in pairs or trios and ask them to list the good and bad effects of using selected appliances. Allow groups to share and discuss their findings in a large group setting.

To enrich student learning, direct children to gather more information about the advantages and disadvantages of using selected appliances from experts around the school and neighborhood. After facts and opinions have been collected, help students examine the information carefully, drawing conclusions about its reliability and generalizability. Then compile a master list of valid pros and cons and reach class consensus on whether the advantages of using these aids outweigh the disadvantages.

ACTIVITY 4. The titles for this chapter do not reference closed-captioning, and children may not realize that TV stations frequently provide this service. You might **make children aware of closed-captioning for hearing-impaired people** by taking a field trip to a nearby television station. To prepare for the visit, help children generate questions that reveal (1) whether or not closed-captioning is available in your area; (2) how hearing-impaired people arrange to receive this service; (3) what devices, if any, must be attached to the television; and (4) how much this service costs. To follow up the field trip, debrief children thoroughly in a class conversation, then ask students to record their new understandings in their social studies journals.

Activities of the Hand: Building Citizenship Skills

ACTIVITY 1. To **boost students' ability to communicate ideas nonverbally**, read *The Day We Met Cindy, A Very Special Friend, I Have a Sister—My Sister Is Deaf, Handtalk Birthday, Buffy's Orange Leash*, and other appropriate titles. As class discussion begins, note that story characters often communicate complicated ideas without uttering a word; then have children list these modes of communication (e.g., signing, finger spelling, lip-reading, body language) on a large sheet of butcher paper. Because children can learn signing fairly easily, invite an expert signer to teach the class a song or poem. Encourage students to demonstrate their new skill at a PTA meeting or school program. If there is adequate time, individual students might learn additional songs and poems, giving presentations to classmates.

ACTIVITY 2. This activity also **promotes students' communication skills as well as allowing them to experiment with nontraditional forms of information processing**. As you share *Through Grandpa's Eyes* in class, children may notice that Grandpa reads with his wife and grandson one afternoon under an apple tree. Be sure they grasp that he is reading a Braille book. To give children additional experiences with this form of communication, locate items printed in Braille such as books, magazines, and alphabet cards as well as equipment for imprinting, such as a Braillewriter. So students can appreciate the degree to which visually impaired persons depend on alternative senses, they can try reading Braille print with only their sense of touch and share their reactions to this means of communication with classmates.

To extend the activity, have children brainstorm public places in which Braille signs and labels enable citizens to function safely (e.g., elevators, rest rooms, phone booths). Inform or remind students that, in some communities, high-pitched sounds are emitted at busy street corners to assist blind pedestrians. Let small groups survey the neighborhood for examples of similar assistance given blind or deaf people and report their findings to the class.

Activities of the Heart: Building Citizenship Dispositions

ACTIVITY 1. To **encourage empathy for visually impaired people**, help children realize how the loss of sight might make a person feel. As you read aloud selected stories that examine blindness (e.g., *Through Grandpa's Eyes, The Gift, A Cane in Her Hand, My Favorite Place, See You Tomorrow, Charles*, and *The Seal Oil Lamp*), ask students to note feelings that visually impaired characters display. Initially, have pairs or trios list these emotions, then combine group ideas to generate a master list on the chalkboard. Dialogue about these feelings with the class, exploring the likelihood that students would share them if faced with a similar handicap.

For enrichment, pair children and alternately blindfold each partner so she or he can experiment with loss of sight and the feelings that this experience generates. While blindfolded, students might describe an object using touch, smell, and hearing. Or they might try to maneuver around a room, building, or playground. Because such activity involves some risk, ensure that blindfolded children are operating in an extremely safe environment. For example, place an adult or trustworthy upper-grade student nearby so that participants do not injure themselves. After blindfolds are removed, ask students to share the feelings they had while blindfolded. Provide additional time for children to compare and contrast their emotions with the list of characters' feelings.

ACTIVITY 2. This teaching idea encourages students to **consider how they would interact with a close friend who is visually impaired**. Read *The Gift* or *Happy Birthday, Grampie*, then pose a few questions to stimulate children's reactions. For example, how might blindness influence the quantity or quality of interactions with a friend? If the friend is not their same age, would they or should they communicate differently? If blindness was a sudden thing, would they worry, as Anna did in *The Gift*, that the nature of the relationship might change? To practice the written as well as the spoken word, have students draft a letter to a real friend, a pretend buddy, or a story character who is visually impaired (see page 74). If possible, they might try printing a few words in Braille. Recruit adults and older students to assist as necessary.

Ph.5. Students examining globe through touch. *(Cliff Sears, Ryan Johnson, Lauren Mardis, Nathen Andreasen, Steven Sullivan, Ashley Livingston)*

To extend the activity, ask children to **think about how they would interact with a hearing-impaired friend.** Read *The Day We Met Cindy*, *A Very Special Friend*, or other appropriate titles. Have the children practice signing familiar words and attempt a simple conversation with a deaf friend, real or imaginary, using only sign language.

ACTIVITY 3. Although most selections for this chapter are works of fiction, they **prompt real emotions and attitudes that help children better appreciate people with disabilities.** After sharing an appropriate title, acquaint students with famous people who exemplify the degree to which persons with handicaps can achieve civic competence. Examples include Helen Keller, Ludwig von Beethoven, Ray Charles, Stevie Wonder, Franklin D. Roosevelt, Yankees pitcher Jim Abbott, and U.S. Senator Bob Dole. Students can conduct research studies, locating photographs or drawings of these people and identifying their accomplishments.

Within their own neighborhood, students may know a citizen who was disabled in military service or in an on-the-job accident. They may have a friend or relative who was injured in a car wreck or born with a disabling condition. As children relate these personal stories in a class conversation, help them understand that a person can exercise productive citizenship, even if her or his body does not work the way it should.

Dear Elizabeth,

I am so sorry about what happened.

Your Mother told me the whole story.
I hope you feel better.
Would you like me to read a story to you?

Your friend,
Maria M. M.

Fig. 9. Sample letter to a visually-impaired friend. *(Maria Macia, age 8)*

Section 4

Diversity in Terms of Ethnicity—
Many Cultures Enrich American Life

For young children to appreciate ethnic diversity, teachers and librarians, as well as parents and community leaders, must retell collected stories from the many cultures that enrich our society. Through quality works of literature, children can interpret the triumphs and tragedies of the African-American experience (chapter 10). They can learn about the major contributions that Asian-Americans have made to our way of life (chapter 11). They can build their knowledge of and respect for Hispanic-American culture in the past, present, and future (chapter 12). Finally, young citizens can hear powerful stories that increase their awareness of the ways in which the Native American nations have influenced American history (chapter 13). As they read stories from many cultures and respond with their own, children can develop the wisdom, skills, and attitudes of civic competence in a diverse and changing world.

Chapter 10

The African-American Experience—
A Culture Born of Triumph and Tragedy

Chapter 10 illuminates the African-American experience, from pioneer home-steads and urban factories in the past to far-ranging occupations and varied locales in the present. Teachers, librarians, and students can examine this rich cultural heritage and profit considerably from their collective efforts. Literature for the primary grades offers important lessons about the rights and responsibilities that young people have inherited as citizens. *Aunt Flossie's Hats (and Crab Cakes Later)*, our featured title, encourages a deeper understanding of the strong family ties and respect for tradition that have carried black culture through triumph and tragedy. Our alternate and related titles suggest a wealth of teaching options that enhance the chapter theme.

Feature Title

Aunt Flossie's Hats (and Crab Cakes Later) by Elizabeth Fitzgerald Howard. Illus. by James Ransome. New York: Clarion Books, 1991. 32p. ISBN 0-395-54682-6.

For Sarah and Susan, visiting Aunt Flossie's house is a special event because she has so many stories to tell! The girls dig through hat boxes, finding numerous treasures from the near and distant past. With each discovery, Aunt Flossie sits back, closes her eyes, revives old memories of Baltimore, and transmits these images across the generations.

Naturally and without pretension, Howard's story introduces classroom experiences that can generate important citizenship learnings. The book portrays a close-knit extended family and offers glimpses of happenings long ago. Children get the chance to compare and contrast "then" with "now" and to gain some of Aunt Flossie's reverence for history. Finally, Howard's work incorporates traditional storytelling techniques, prompting opportunities to increase children's social and communication skills.

Alternate Titles

Ben's Trumpet by Rachel Isadora. New York: Greenwillow Books, 1979. 32p. ISBN 0-688-80194-3.

Little Ben dreams constantly about trumpets. He believes so totally that he will play a horn one day that the neighbor kids begin muttering that he is crazy. A chance meeting transforms Ben's vision into reality when a professional musician offers the boy an opportunity to belt out a few notes on his shiny trumpet.

Isadora's story features jazz artistry—a source of considerable accomplishment and deserved pride for the African-American community. Ben leads primary readers through a musical environment that they might investigate at length. The boy also reveals patience and persistence as he pursues his aspirations, qualities that young citizens might well take to heart.

The Black Snowman by Phil Mendez. Illus. by Carol Byard. New York: Scholastic, 1989. 48p. ISBN 0-590-40552-7.

Mendez's touching Christmas story blends historical reality with hopeful fantasy. Jacob, a boy from the inner city, struggles with being poor and black. He discovers an African *kente* cloth and magically summons a black snowman, whose wondrous gifts let the boy build self-esteem and reach an accommodation with his difficult circumstances.

Mendez transmits clear and powerful messages that parallel major goals for most social-studies curricula. As they observe Jacob sensing the power of his African ancestry, all children can achieve self-awareness, grow in self-worth, and gain a sense of efficacy in their daily lives. Black children should find these themes particularly meaningful. Children might also build critical thinking and communication skills as they dialogue about the book's main ideas.

Irene and the Big, Fine Nickel by Irene Smalls-Hector. Illus. by Tyrone Geter. Boston: Little, Brown, 1991. 32p. ISBN 0-316-79871-1.

Living in Harlem in the 1950s, a girl is enjoying a typical Saturday morning playing with her close friends when the three girls find a nickel in the street.

Smalls-Hector transports today's children to a place and time that most would not otherwise experience. Her story affords a chance to observe family and friends working and playing together in a vibrant, close-knit black community. The book also provides opportunities to analyze shifting values as children visit an age when a nickel was much more valuable than it is now.

Related Titles

Black Is Brown Is Tan by Arnold Adoff. Illus. by Emily McCully. New York: HarperCollins, 1973. 32p. ISBN 0-060-20084-7.

In verse, Adoff depicts a biracial family doing what any family loves to do—playing together in the snow, reading lots of books, singing favorite songs, and welcoming a visit from relatives.

Black Like Kyra, White Like Me by Judith Vigna. Morton Grove, IL: A. Whitman, 1992. 32p. ISBN 0-807-50778-4.

The narrator, a white girl, rejoices when a black friend and her family move next door. But trouble occurs almost immediately as white neighbors show their prejudice. Although the discourse seems somewhat shallow at times, the story does perform a valuable service—introducing a troubling issue in terms that young children might understand.

Bright Eyes, Brown Skin by Cheryl W. Hudson and Bernette G. Ford. Illus. by George Ford. Orange, NJ: Just Us Books, 1990. 24p. ISBN 0-940-97510-6.

In this installment of the Feeling Good series, rhyming text and colorful visuals capture the mood as four young friends make the most of an otherwise uneventful school day.

Charlie Parker Played Be Bop by Chris Raschka. New York: Orchard Books, 1992. 32p. ISBN 0-531-08599-6.

The author uses few words and powerful illustrations to acquaint children with "Bird" Parker, the saxophonist who made *bebop* a household word.

Cherries and Cherry Pits by Vera B. Williams. New York: Greenwillow Books, 1986. 40p. ISBN 0-688-05146-4.

Bidemmi draws pictures and tells stories about four residents of her urban neighborhood. Otherwise very diverse, her characters share one common trait—a love for cherries. Bidemmi's own story carries a citizenship message beyond eating fruit—she will plant the pits and grow cherry trees to beautify her community.

Chita's Christmas Tree by Elizabeth Fitzgerald Howard. Illus. by Floyd Cooper. New York: Bradbury Press, 1989. 32p. ISBN 0-027-44621-2.

In a story set in Baltimore at the turn of this century, Chita and her father leave the city to pick a Christmas tree. He marks the tree with Chita's name and insists that Santa will deliver it to their home.

Clean Your Room, Harvey Moon! by Pat Cummings. New York: Bradbury Press, 1991. 32p. ISBN 0-027-25511-5.

In this humorous story told in verse, Harvey learns a valuable civic lesson—rights carry responsibilities—as he must clean his room before he can watch cartoons.

Cornrows by Camille Yarbrough. Illus. by Carole Byard. New York: Coward, McCann & Geoghegan, 1979. 48p. ISBN 0-698-20529-4.

As they braid Sister's and Brother's hair, Mama and Great-Grammaw explain the origin of cornrows, stressing that these designs symbolize strength and courage.

Elijah's Angel: A Story for Chanukah and Christmas by Michael J. Rosen. Illus. by Aminah Brenda Lynn Robinson. San Diego, CA: Harcourt Brace Jovanovich, 1992. 32p. ISBN 0-152-25394-7.

An 80-year-old black barber gives a young Jewish boy an unforgettable Christmas present, a striking, hand-carved angel. In return, the nine-year-old presents his friend with a Chanukah gift, the menorah that he made in Hebrew school. Their gift exchange shows that friendship can transcend religious and racial differences.

Go Fish by Mary Stolz. Illus. by Pat Cummings. New York: HarperCollins, 1991. 74p. ISBN 0-060-25822-5.

In this easy-to-read sequel to *Storm in the Night* (a chapter 1 title), Thomas and his grandfather spend time fishing, telling whoppers, and enjoying each other's company.

Joshua's Masai Mask by Dakari Hru. Illus. by Anna Rich. New York: Lee & Low Books, 1993. 32p. ISBN 1-880-00002-4.

Joshua fears that classmates will tease him if he plays the kalimba in the school talent show. To get him into the spirit for playing, an uncle loans Joshua a Masai mask with unexpected magical powers. Inspired to give a stirring public performance, Joshua gains self-confidence and realizes his self-worth.

Kimako's Story by June Jordan. Boston: Houghton Mifflin, 1991. 48p. ISBN 0-395-60338-2 (paper).

Seven-year-old Kimako is a curious girl. She likes to explore her neighborhood, read, and make up poem-puzzles—activities that young readers might also enjoy.

Li'l Sis and Uncle Willie: A Story Based on the Life and Paintings of William H. Johnson by Gwen Everett. Illus. by William H. Johnson. New York: Rizzoli, 1991. 32p. ISBN 0-847-81462-9.

Everett chronicles the life of an African-American artist through the eyes of his almost-six-year-old niece. Johnson's paintings enliven this unusual and thoughtful book.

Masai and I by Virginia Kroll. Illus. by Nancy Carpenter. New York: Four Winds Press, 1992. 32p. ISBN 0-027-51165-0.

Linda, a young city girl, studies East Africa in school. One day her imagination carries her there, so she can visualize how the Masai live.

Mirandy and Brother Wind by Patricia McKissack. Illus. by Jerry Pinkney. New York: Alfred A. Knopf, 1988. 32p. ISBN 0-394-98765-9.

Set in an early twentieth-century rural black community, the story relates how Mirandy, Ezel, and Brother Wind win the junior cakewalk competition. McKissack, incidentally, was inspired by a photo of her grandparents winning a cakewalk contest as teenagers.

My First Kwanzaa Book by Deborah M. Newton Chocolate. Illus. by Cal Massey. New York: Scholastic, 1992. 26p. ISBN 0-590-45762-4.

This storybook introduces children to Kwanzaa, the African-American holiday established formally in 1966.

Nancy No-Size by Mary Hoffman. Illus. by Jennifer Northway. New York: Oxford University Press, 1987. 26p. ISBN 0-195-20596-0.

After many frustrating moments, Nancy finds her special place as the middle child in a biracial family.

Never Fear, Flip the Dip Is Here by Philip Hanft. Illus. by Thomas B. Allen. New York: Dial Press, 1991. 32p. ISBN 0-803-70897-1.

Neighborhood children pick on Flip because he has hardly any baseball skills. With his father away in the Navy, he turns to Buster, a black, former minor league player, to learn the game.

The Skates of Uncle Richard by Carol Fenner. Illus. by Ati Forberg. New York: Random House, 1978. 48p. ISBN 0-394-93553-5.

With her uncle's encouragement, a nine-year-old girl takes the first steps toward realizing her dream—becoming a figure skater.

Tar Beach by Faith Ringgold. New York: Crown, 1991. 32p. ISBN 0-517-58031-4.

It's Harlem in the summer of 1939, and Cassie Louise Lightfoot lies on the roof of her building—what the neighbors call "tar beach"—and dreams of flying. Ringgold bases this award-winning book on her acclaimed story quilt of the same name.

Tell Me a Story, Mama by Angela Johnson. Illus. by David Soman. New York: Orchard, 1988. 32p. ISBN 0-531-08394-2.

In this warm family story, Mama shares her favorite childhood tales with an eager listener, her young daughter.

Three Wishes by Lucille Clifton. Illus. by Michael Hays. New York: Doubleday, 1992. 32p. ISBN 0-385-30497-8.

Finding a lucky penny, Nobie makes three wishes on it. The result is an argument that ruins her friendship with Victorius. After a heart-to-heart with her mother, Nobie wishes that she "still had a good friend."

Wagon Wheels by Barbara Brenner. Illus. by Don Bolognese. New York: HarperCollins, 1978. 64p. ISBN 0-060-20669-1.

Based on true incidents involving settlers and American Indians, Brenner recounts a black family's travels from Kentucky to a Kansas homestead after the Civil War.

What Will Mommy Do When I'm at School? by Dolores Johnson. New York: Macmillan, 1990. 32p. ISBN 0-027-47845-9.

With school starting the next day, a child worries about how her mother can ever manage without her.

Wild Wild Sunflower Child Anna by Nancy White Carlstrom. Illus. by Jerry Pinkney. New York: Macmillan, 1987. 32p. ISBN 0-027-17360-7.

Romping happily through the great outdoors, Anna displays exuberance, joy, and imagination in great abundance.

Teaching Options

Read aloud *Aunt Flossie's Hats (and Crab Cakes Later)* or any of the other titles cited in this chapter, then try one or more of the following teaching ideas. Most activities are not tailored to specific titles, although they may produce more interesting results with some books than others. As with preceding chapters, we encourage you to modify any of these ideas to fit your teaching situation and adjust them to accommodate multiple titles.

The sensitive, sometimes controversial nature of our chapter theme demands that you follow our First Commandment of elementary teaching: **Know thy students.** Particular books may strike an emotional cord within individual students. We remember, for example, the African-American fifth-grader who cried openly during a rendering of *Nettie's Trip South* by Ann Turner (Macmillan, 1987), explaining later that he "just got mad" whenever he thought about slavery. Clearly, you cannot always anticipate the meaning that a child will make from a particular story. At the same time, be prepared to deal with deeply personal reactions in a caring, appropriate manner.

Activities of the Head: Building Citizenship Understandings

ACTIVITY 1. Through many of this chapter's story selections, children can **discover or reinforce the important contributions that African-Americans have made to the arts.** After reading *Ben's Trumpet* or *Charlie Parker Played Be Bop*, help children **investigate the African-American influence on music**, especially jazz forms. Let them find photos and bits of information about jazz greats, including Duke Ellington, Scott Joplin, Ella Fitzgerald, Louis Armstrong, Charlie Parker, Sarah Vaughn, Count Basie, Miles Davis, Wynton and Branford Marsalis, Lionel Hampton, Anita Baker, and Quincy Jones. Take class time to listen to their music and, if possible, watch videotapes of their performances. To conclude, ask the class to select a favorite jazz musician or piece of music or both.

As an alternate or complementary approach, **acquaint children with African-American influences in the dance world.** Read aloud *Mirandy and Brother Wind*, then hold a brief class conversation about the origin of the cakewalk. Dialogue about the ways in which black styles have influenced contemporary American dance. Compare and contrast cakewalking, as well as such traditional styles as square dancing or the jitterbug, with current dance trends. Encourage the children to try some different dance steps, including Michael Jackson's moon walk or hip hop street dancing. To augment your own knowledge and skill level, invite a local expert to demonstrate these styles in the classroom.

If time permits you to go beyond music and dance, use *Li'l Sis and Uncle Willie: A Story Based on the Life and Paintings of William H. Johnson* to **introduce similar experiences probing the African-American impact on the visual arts.**

ACTIVITY 2. A wise old educator once stated that play is the vocation of youngsters. To help students **grasp the nature and power of play,** share stories that depict people having fun and trying interesting, if not always practical endeavors. Use the listed titles to exemplify African-Americans enjoying themselves in constructive, productive ways, for example, Mirandy dancing; Ben playing the trumpet; Irene competing in games with friends; Chita enjoying traditional holiday experiences; Uncle Richard skating; Elijah carving angels; Sister, Brother, and

Kimako having their hair done while listening to stories. After reading and discussing these stories, ask class members to talk with grandparents or parents or both about games and other fun things they remember playing and doing as children.

When students have awakened their interest and increased their understanding about play in a general sense, help them list specific nonwork activities that they might like to try. Then let children form small groups according to their interests. Ask the media specialist and adult volunteers to help them **gather important information** about preferred activities (e.g., skills needed to perform them, directions or rules to follow, necessary materials, and space and time requirements). Check the accuracy of children's research, then encourage them to try these activities during recess, in special classes, or at home.

Enrich children's study of play by helping them organize a **Multicultural Fun Day** involving multiple classrooms or even the whole school. Invite parents and grandparents to assist with some of the events, which might include a cakewalk, a fiddling contest, food tasting, ethnic dancing, games from around the world, a limbo contest, hair styling, and storytelling. Allow time during this day for children to demonstrate their preferred activities and share new understandings about play.

ACTIVITY 3. Read and discuss several of the listed titles, then **broaden children's understanding of African-American culture** by inviting a speaker to share her or his expertise with the class. Encourage the guest to examine age-appropriate topics and issues (e.g., cornrowing hair, quilting, storytelling, Kwanzaa traditions), to demonstrate customs and practices whenever possible, and to answer questions that children have generated in advance.

ACTIVITY 4. This activity promotes students' comprehension of a common topic in primary social studies programs: **the comparison of city life with country life**. In small or large group settings, read aloud *Irene and the Big, Fine Nickel*, *The Black Snowman*, *Cherries and Cherry Pits*, *Elijah's Angel*, *Tar Beach* and other stories to elaborate the details of urban living. Share *Mirandy and Brother Wind*, *Tell Me a Story, Mama*, and *Wild Wild Sunflower Child Anna* to depict a more rural lifestyle. Then have children record everything they recollect about each setting on a two-column chart. Divide children into small groups to compare and contrast these ways of life. To conclude, brainstorm the advantages and disadvantages of city versus country living in a whole-class meeting. Ask each student to determine the setting that he or she would prefer and illustrate that choice in a drawing or collage.

For older primary students, *Wagon Wheels* can add a time dimension to this activity. After reading and reviewing the story, let children compare and contrast city and country life as they existed many years ago. To reinforce student understanding, create a class mural illustrating urban and rural lifestyles in pioneer times.

Activities of the Hand: Building Citizenship Skills

ACTIVITY 1. In this activity, children **tackle a solvable problem and make design decisions** while creating quilt squares. They should also **gain confidence and better appreciate the effort that a crafts project often demands.** To begin, read aloud Faith Ringgold's imaginative story *Tar Beach*, animating a quilt that depicts life in Harlem 50 years ago. Display the book and provide time for each child to scrutinize Ringgold's intricate illustrations.

Fig. 10. A self-portrait quilt square. *(Andy McGowan, age 5)*

Convene a class meeting and propose a project, constructing a quilt from high-quality paper or un-bleached muslin. Determine a multicultural theme for the artwork, perhaps a depiction of neighborhood life, a look "Beyond Tar Beach" or "Tar Beach II, the Sequel," a picture-biography of famous African-Americans, or self-portraits of each person in the class.

Outline a work schedule and en-sure that each student grasps her or his responsibility, that is, making a quilt square that reflects the project theme. Appoint a committee to coor-dinate class efforts and, with adult supervision, combine individual squares into a final product. Once the quilt is finished, prominently dis-play the artwork in your school.

To add a citizenship dimension, consider giving the class project to a small child who could really use a warm cover, assuming that the class has made a durable, cloth quilt. Check with homeless shelters or lo-cal religious organizations in your area for possible recipients.

ACTIVITY 2. This activity **builds students' social and communica-tion skills, and also promotes their understanding of the importance of recording customs and tradi-tions for future generations.** Begin by advising students that past cul-tures preserved valuable traditions through visual means; in modern times, tech-nological societies typically employ photography. Then share stories that feature visual records of cultural information. For example, the author bases *Mirandy and Brother Wind* on a photo of her grandparents. *Aunt Flossie's Hats, Ben's Trumpet, Tar Beach, Elijah's Angel, My First Kwanzaa Book,* and *Cherries and Cherry Pits* portray African-American traditions through vivid illustrations. Read and discuss as many titles as possible, then ask class members to choose a favorite tradition picture from each story. Examine these visuals carefully, noting distinctive elements that make them valuable reservoirs of cultural knowledge.

Next, give students an interactive homework assignment. Have them ask parents or grandparents to locate a photo that captures an important family tradition, and bring the picture to school. Let them discuss their photos in small or large group settings. Additionally, children could caption the photos, collect them in a notebook ("Family Traditions of Our Class"), and share this volume with other classes.

ACTIVITY 3. Through this chapter's story selections, many characters learn traditions from their elders (e.g., *Elijah's Angel, Go Fish, Cornrows, Aunt Flossie's Hats, Tell Me a Story, Mama*). After reading several books aloud, introduce this activity to **promote oral and written communication skills as well as students' appreciation of cultural traditions and values**. Encourage children to preserve their families' traditions by asking older relatives to write them in story form or record them on audiotape or videotape. If the class is culturally mixed, the activity should generate a rich collection of tradition stories that students might share in pairs or trios. To conclude, each child can retell her or his tradition story in writing, with assistance as necessary. Combine these vignettes into a class booklet for display in the media center.

ACTIVITY 4. To improve students' research skills and further expand their cultural horizons, ask them to search magazines and newspapers, particularly ethnic publications such as *Hispanic* or *Ebony*, for pictures of people from various cultures, particularly African-Americans. Have small groups combine their photos and construct a collage that portrays people from various backgrounds working together harmoniously. Each child can then write or dictate a story to accompany the visual. Encourage children to develop personalities and imagine daily routines for the people in their pictures, or to project themselves as particular characters, or both.

As a variation, you might ask each child to choose a character from one of the chapter 10 titles. After drawing this person, encourage students to write a story describing an encounter with him or her.

Activities of the Heart: Building Citizenship Dispositions

ACTIVITY 1. Hearing a storyteller transmit his or her cultural traditions can **promote children's empathy for people with diverse ethnic backgrounds and different ways of life**. After reading a variety of selections, especially *Cornrows, Cherries and Cherry Pits, Aunt Flossie's Hats,* and *Tell Me a Story, Mama,* invite an African-American storyteller to visit your school. Often, media specialists and public librarians have established contacts with storytellers reflecting diverse ethnic traditions. These professionals can also suggest collections of stories, media, and educational materials with which to follow up the visit.

ACTIVITY 2. This activity targets an important goal of most primary grade social studies programs: **fostering the qualities that encourage the empathetic, interpersonal dimensions of citizenship, for example, seeing other viewpoints, developing self-awareness and self-concept, and respecting cultural**

differences. Many titles listed here feature characters modeling these traits, such as *The Black Snowman, Nancy No-Size, Masai and I, Joshua's Masai Mask, Black Is Brown Is Tan,* and *Black Like Kyra, White Like Me.* Reading one or more of these stories should spark a class conversation about cultural differences, human commonalities, personal pride, and the most productive ways to treat others. Help children consider why people look and act differently, and what this world would be like if everyone looked and acted the same. Ask students to brainstorm ways that people are different on the outside but alike on the inside; then generate a class list of feelings, thoughts, and needs that everyone possesses. Conclude by creating small group pictures that exhibit ways to show cultural appreciation as we interact with others in school and across our diverse world.

ACTIVITY 3. To **improve children's self-esteem and self-confidence in social situations**, let them compare and contrast their dreams, aspirations, and desires with the visions of characters in selected stories, for example, *Kimako's Story, Cornrows, Ben's Trumpet,* and *The Skates of Uncle Richard.* Like most primary-age children, these characters verbalize desires and wishes for the future. Help students realize that everyone has such dreams. Lead them to the conclusion that children living in different locations and young people with varied cultural backgrounds share similar visions and aspirations. Have children illustrate their dreams, sharing them in small groups, if comfortable enough to do so.

To extend the activity, reexamine *Cornrows'* impressionistic pictures and text, searching for author references to many famous black people, including Dr. Martin Luther King, Jr., Harriet Tubman, Rosa Parks, Harry Belafonte, Aretha Franklin, Josephine Baker, and Langston Hughes. Then help older primary students gather information about the dreams of these people, illustrating their research and sharing their findings in creative ways.

Chapter 11

The Asian-American Experience—
Listening and Learning

This chapter concentrates on the lives of Asian-Americans, people who came from many different cultures and nations, arriving generations ago and as recently as yesterday. Listening to and learning from their stories can positively influence the civic understandings, skills, and dispositions of young citizens. In the varied titles cited in this chapter, teachers, librarians, and students will find a wealth of possibilities for listening and learning. We chose a particularly informative book as the feature title: *Cleversticks*, a lighthearted story about a boy who tries to find his own special skill. The alternate and related titles provide additional opportunities to listen and learn about the peoples who immigrated to this country from Asia.

Feature Title

Cleversticks by Bernard Ashley. Illus. by Derek Brazell. New York: Crown, 1992. 32p. ISBN 0-517-58879-X.

Ling Sung wishes that he could be clever at something. His classmates can tie their own shoes, write their names, and button their sweaters without having an extra button left at the bottom. After many disappointments, his friends notice him wielding two paintbrushes like chopsticks and clamor to learn how to use "cleversticks," too.

As they observe Ling Sung's diverse classroom, young readers can witness social studies learnings applied in a real-life setting. They can perceive, for example, a boy's quest for a sense of belonging and achievement; they can identify the ways in which he builds self-esteem and self-confidence; they can acquire and practice the social skills to develop and sustain childhood relationships.

Alternate Titles

Aekyung's Dream by Min Paek. Rev. ed. San Francisco: Children's Book Press, 1988. 24p. ISBN 0-892-39042-5.

Aekyung, a shy Korean girl who has recently arrived in this country, has trouble adjusting to her new school. Classmates call her "Chinese," a label she cannot accept because she is Korean. With much effort and reflective thought, she overcomes her fears, employing her talent as a painter to communicate and find common ground with her peers.

Characters in Paek's bilingual story (written in English and Korean) model important social studies skills in action. They struggle to deal with different points of view; they discover and adopt alternative modes of communication; and, as their bank of common experiences increases, they develop positive skills for social interaction.

Angel Child, Dragon Child by Michele Maria Surat. Illus. by Vo-Dinh Mai. Milwaukee, WI: Raintree, 1983. 32p. ISBN 0-940-74212-8.

This title also involves the frustrations and homesickness of a young Asian girl adapting to life in this country. Although she resembles Aekyung in many ways, Ut has an additional problem. Most of her family came with her to the United States, but her mother remained in Vietnam. Curiously, Ut's fight with a schoolmate opens the door for mutual understanding and provides a touching ending to the story.

Children can compare and contrast the social situations that Aekyung and Ut face as new immigrants to the United States. Although both girls search for acceptance, they achieve their ends by different means. Additionally, Ut's background introduces children to a conflict that had a major impact on recent American history and a geographic region that reappears frequently in the headlines.

Roses Sing on New Snow: A Delicious Tale by Paul Yee. Illus. by Harvey Chan. New York: Macmillan, 1991. 32p. ISBN 0-027-93622-8.

In Chinatown during the early 1900s, Maylin is the chief cook in her father's restaurant, but her brothers receive all the credit. When a government official insists that a delicacy be prepared in his presence, Maylin finally receives the recognition that she has long deserved.

Yee's humorous story about a turn-of-the-century Chinese-American family provides children a chance to savor the sights, sounds, and flavors of a past age. Young readers can also analyze the customs and traditions of an Asian culture, particularly the maintenance of unequal social status for young men and women. Additionally, students might hone their abilities to follow directions in a cooking exercise.

Related Titles

A to Zen: A Book of Japanese Culture by Ruth Wells. Illus. by Yoshi. Saxonville, MA: Picture Book Studio, 1992. ISBN 0-88708-175-4.

More than an alphabet book, this series of brief stories reveals much information about ancient and modern Japan. Entries follow alphabetical order, with the exception of the letters *L, Q, V,* and *X,* which have no corresponding sounds in Japanese.

Chang's Paper Pony by Eleanor Coerr. Illus. by Deborah K. Ray. New York: HarperCollins, 1988. 32p. ISBN 0-060-021329-9.

Coerr treats the loneliness and discomfort that accompany immigration in this story about a Chinese boy who reaches America during the California Gold Rush. Although the 1840s setting may confuse younger children, older primary students may be ready for an introductory look at the period.

Chinese Eyes by Marjorie Ann Waybill. Illus. by Pauline Cutrell. Scottdale, PA: Herald Press, 1974. 34p. ISBN 0-836-11738-7.

When a third-grade classmate calls an adopted Korean girl "Chinese eyes," her mother helps her deal with his taunts. Mother and daughter compare their own eyes and conclude that the only thing that matters is the ability to see well.

Emma's Dragon Hunt by Catherine Stock. New York: Lothrop, Lee & Shepard, 1984. 32p. ISBN 0-688-02698-2.

Grandfather Wong, a recent arrival from China, introduces Emma to dragon lore. Frightened at the thought of dragons dancing on her roof, the young girl is reassured after Grandfather explains what dragons mean in Chinese mythology.

Everybody Cooks Rice by Norah Dooley. Illus. by Peter J. Thornton. Minneapolis, MN: Carolrhoda Books, 1991. 32p. ISBN 0-876-14412-1.

Carrie visits families from Barbados, Vietnam, India, China, and Haiti as she searches for her brother up and down the block. Everybody is having rice for supper. Returning home, she discovers her mother making *risi e bisi* from a family recipe. Incidentally, the author includes recipes for every dish mentioned in the story.

The First Snow by Helen Coutant. Illus. by Vo-Dinh Mai. New York: Alfred A. Knopf, 1974. 36p. ISBN 0-394-92831-8.

Recent emigrants from Vietnam, a girl and her sick grandmother discuss the Buddhist life-and-death cycle. Grandmother uses the metaphor of "the first snow" to show Lien that she may seem to die but will actually live in a different form. Although interesting and informative, the story seems too complex for very young children.

Grandfather Tang's Story by Ann Tompert. Illus. by Robert Andrew Parker. New York: Crown, 1990. 32p. ISBN 0-517-57272-9.

Tompert introduces an ancient Chinese puzzle form as she describes Grandfather telling Little Soo about shape-changing fox fairies. Puzzle shapes called tangrams figure prominently in the old man's tale and are still used today.

How My Parents Learned to Eat by Ina R. Friedman. Illus. by Allen Say. Boston: Houghton Mifflin, 1987. 30p. ISBN 0-395-35379-3.

A girl recounts the courtship of her mother, a Japanese student, and her father, an American sailor, focusing on their adjustment to different customs in table manners.

I Hate English! by Ellen Levine. Illus. by Steve Bjorkman. New York: Scholastic, 1989. 32p. ISBN 0-590-42305-3.

Mei Mei, a recent emigrant from Hong Kong, seems comfortable in New York but fights learning English. A teacher at the Chinatown Learning Center helps her grasp the utility of being fluent in both languages.

My Best Friend Mee-Yung Kim: Meeting a Korean-American Family by Dianne MacMillan and Dorothy Freeman. Ed. by Jane Steltenpohl. Illus. by Bob Marstall. Englewood Cliffs, NJ: Messner, 1989. 48p. ISBN 0-671-65691-0.

Part of the My Best Friend series, this book offers insights into Korean customs, foods, celebrations, holidays, and more in an appealing and instructive way.

The Paper Crane by Molly Bang. New York: Greenwillow Books, 1985. 32p. ISBN 0-688-04109-4.

Blending Asian folklore and Western settings, Bang describes a restaurant owner who runs a successful business, until a new highway cuts off customers' access. One day the owner feeds a penniless stranger who pays him with a magical origami crane instead of money. People again come to the restaurant to see the bird sing and dance.

Sachiko Means Happiness by Kimiko Sakai. Illus. by Tomie Arai. San Francisco: Children's Book Press, 1990. 32p. ISBN 0-892-39065-4.

Because of Alzheimer's disease, Sachiko's grandmother no longer recognizes her and behaves strangely at times. Although these changes upset the young girl, she soon discovers ways that they can stay happy together.

Tales from Gold Mountain: Stories of the Chinese in the New World by Paul Yee. Illus. by Simon Ng. New York: Macmillan, 1990. 64p. ISBN 0-027-93621-X.

Based on Chinese immigrant experiences in the United States and Canada, Yee's eight short stories emphasize important themes that older primary children can comprehend: the clash between the traditional and the modern, family loyalty despite lengthy separation, exploitation in the workplace, facing hardship and danger, racial discrimination, and perseverance.

Through Moon and Stars and Night Skies by Ann Warren Turner. Illus. by James G. Hale. New York: HarperCollins, 1990. 32p. ISBN 0-060-26190-0.

In this treatment of the culture shock that may accompany transracial adoptions, a young Asian boy reminisces about traveling from his native country to meet his new parents in the United States.

Teaching Options

Introduce these teaching ideas after reading *Cleversticks* or any of the alternate or related titles. As previously noted, most activities do not depend on specific titles but may be better suited to some books than others. Please modify these teaching ideas to fit your situation and incorporate multiple books in a particular activity, allowing children to compare and contrast the many ways in which authors treat a concept or theme.

The intensely personal quality of our chapter theme may strike an emotional cord within individual students. Levine, Coutant, Waybill, and Surat, for example, have crafted works of fiction that might echo the true stories of students in your classroom. Clearly, you cannot anticipate precisely how a child will react to a narrative. Still, know your students well enough that you are prepared to deal with an emotional crisis in a supportive manner.

Activities of the Head: Building Citizenship Understandings

ACTIVITY 1. Connecting spoken language with written language is a process that all children struggle with in their primary years. They may find it difficult to transcribe words that they have only spoken previously. As they examine the Asian-American experience, students can **discover that children from other cultures must learn sets of symbols very different from the ABC's**. Share the story of Mei Mei (*I Hate English!*), who loves to write in Chinese but cannot yet grasp the English alphabet. Read aloud *A to Zen* and learn more about Moji. Let children study the Korean characters in *Aekyung's Dream*, comparing and contrasting them with the English alphabet. If possible, find other Asian language books, newspapers, or comics for class members to view. Finally, invite people who are proficient in one or more of the Asian symbol systems (please note: they vary from country to country) to demonstrate how their written language is used to communicate ideas or record events.

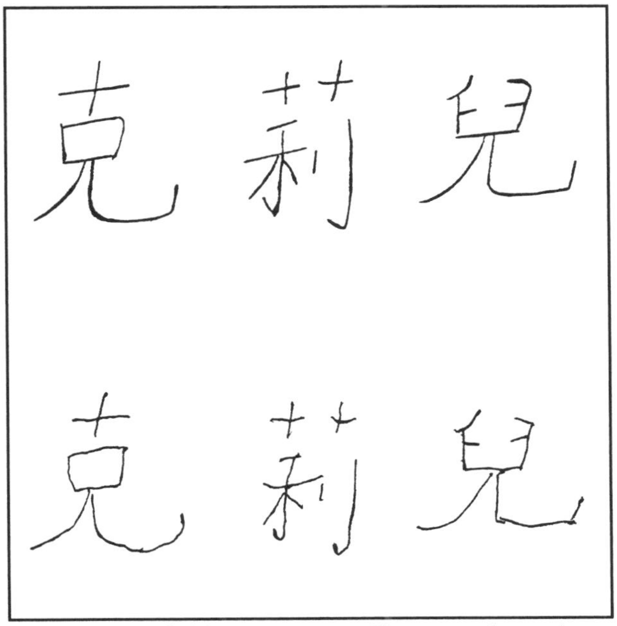

To personalize this experience, ask your guests to write each child's name in characters. The children might try their hand at writing symbols by tracing their names onto another piece of paper or transcribing familiar terms into their journals.

Fig. 11. A child's name in Chinese characters. *(Original by Wei-Chen Sun, graduate student; tracing by Claire McGowan, age 7)*

ACTIVITY 2. To increase students' familiarity with other cultures and with the uncertainties that may arise when changing locales, ask them to ponder how a family move from the United States to China or another Asian country would affect them. After reading *How My Parents Learned to Eat*; *A to Zen*; *Angel Child, Dragon Child*; *Emma's Dragon Hunt*; *I Hate English!*; *Chinese Eyes*; *Through Moon and Stars and Night Skies*; or *Cleversticks*, help children brainstorm some of the differences and similarities they might encounter should they move to Japan, China, Korea, or Vietnam (e.g., food, eating utensils, language, housing, clothing, games). Let children discuss the emotional impact of anticipated changes in small group conversations.

Then arrange visits to the media center for further research, securing adult assistance as student abilities dictate. To conclude, have children make lists in words or pictures of items their families should pack for the move to Asia. Provide time for the class to share this information in some creative way, such as role-playing family members as they prepare for their trip.

ACTIVITY 3. This activity **allows older primary students to realize that exploring the past can encourage a better understanding of the present**. To begin, read and discuss titles that portray Asian-American life in times past, such as *Tales from Gold Mountain: Stories of the Chinese in the New World*, *Chang's Paper Pony*, or *Roses Sing on New Snow: A Delicious Tale*. With assistance, children can work in small groups to construct timelines showing the approximate dates in which the stories took place. They can also review the ways of life that prevailed at each point on the timeline and compare and contrast living conditions then with conditions now. Incidentally, references to topics treated in *A to Zen* might assist students as they make comparisons. They might also find a two-column chart (conditions then versus conditions now) helpful in their deliberations. Finally, a class conversation about their findings should help young people perceive the relationship between past and present.

Activities of the Hand: Building Citizenship Skills

ACTIVITY 1. Chapter 11 titles present tales of people immigrating to the United States from various places in Asia, including Korea (*Aekyung's Dream*, *Chinese Eyes*, and *My Best Friend Mee-Yung Kim*); mainland China (*Emma's Dragon Hunt*, *Tales from Gold Mountain*, *Grandfather Tang's Story*, and *Roses Sing on New Snow*); Japan (*How My Parents Learned to Eat* and *Sachiko Means Happiness*); Hong Kong (*I Hate English!*); and Vietnam (*Angel Child* and *First Snow*). Sharing these books with students **promotes their geographic skills, particularly the ability to determine relative location**. As you read aloud selected titles, have a map and globe handy so student volunteers can locate story settings. Provide clues as necessary. Take time to ensure that class members grasp the location of these places relative to your community or at least to the United States. Typically, this activity motivates children for mini-lessons that reinforce basic geography skills.

For enrichment, ask pairs or trios of students to analyze the essential elements of a journey from selected Asian countries to the United States. To prompt student thinking, ask: How would a family get to the United States from this country? By boat? Plane? How many stops might they make on the way? How long would the trip take? How much might the trip cost? Consider inviting a travel agent to serve as a resource person as students investigate these questions. To conclude, ask the students to outline a proposed journey to the United States in a creative way, such as preparing a travel brochure, writing a letter to a friend, or role-playing a meeting with a travel agent.

ACTIVITY 2. Citizenship requires communication. Citizens young and old receive necessary information from the signs and posters that they encounter continually. Because children seem to recognize that signs serve an important function, reading and constructing these visuals prompt students to **acquire and practice written communication skills**. Have them work in small groups, creating systems of signs that guide young citizens to demonstrate appropriate in-school behaviors. Examples include classroom signs reinforcing good work habits, school-wide visuals reminding children to move in a safe manner, and lunchroom posters restating appropriate table manners. Group children by their interests and help them design eye-catching signs and display them in easy-to-see locations. Finally, select class representatives to publicize the sign systems, traveling from classroom to classroom to explain what the signs mean and why they were made.

ACTIVITY 3. Because they feature ethnic foods and various eating utensils, titles like *Cleversticks, How My Parents Learned to Eat, Everybody Cooks Rice, Roses Sing on New Snow: A Delicious Tale, The Paper Crane,* and *My Best Friend Mee-Yung Kim* can introduce experiences that **promote children's social skills, particularly their ability to interact productively at mealtime**. The titles also **increase their awareness of foods and utensils from various cultures.**

Begin by collecting recipes from the families of Asian-American students or from cookbooks or both. A parent volunteer might prepare sample dishes or help small groups of students cook several of the recipes. Then host an Asian food party in which students and special guests can consume their efforts. Before the event, review proper table etiquette in Asian countries, consulting titles such as *A to Zen, Cleversticks,* and *How My Parents Learned to Eat* for guidance. If possible, invite Asian-American adults or students to assist children as they wield possibly unfamiliar utensils. Provide class time for students to react to the experience in their journals and share their impressions in a class conversation.

ACTIVITY 4. Many cultures transmit knowledge about toys, puzzles, and games from generation to generation. *Grandfather Tang's Story* models this process as Grandfather introduces Little Soo to an ancient but still used Chinese puzzle form, the tangram. The book and this accompanying activity encourage children to **hone listening and problem-solving skills as they discover the secret of tangrams and practice making them**.

Start by giving students the seven *tans* (puzzle pieces) used in the story (five triangles, one square, and one parallelogram). Group children in pairs or trios and have them name the various shapes, then re-create Grandfather's animals. Reread the story as necessary. If students seem interested, let them piece together other tangrams and draft short stories to explain their creations.

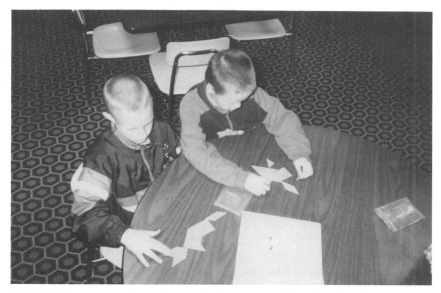

Ph.6. Children experimenting with tangrams. *(Eric Krackenburger, Eric Stidman)*

Activities of the Heart: Building Citizenship Dispositions

ACTIVITY 1. In some titles, characters have recently arrived in the United States from Asian countries and find themselves in uncomfortable situations that cause fear, worry, or unhappiness. Examples include *Through Moon and Stars and Night Skies*; *Aekyung's Dream*; *Angel Child, Dragon Child*; *I Hate English!*; and *Chinese Eyes*. Reading and dialoguing about these stories can help children **appreciate why it seems difficult to meet people, make friends, and feel comfortable in unfamiliar surroundings.**

Read aloud several titles, then ask students to brainstorm uncomfortable situations in which they might find themselves, such as changing schools, attending a different place of worship, joining a ball team, or moving to a new neighborhood. Help children establish the feelings that these settings might generate and identify reasons why these emotions are largely negative. Let students work in small groups to develop actions that they can take to overcome the upsets that unfamiliar situations bring. Carry the conversation a step further by listing actions the children can take to help other newcomers overcome their fears. Finally, determine ways that your students can implement these recommendations on a regular basis.

ACTIVITY 2. Invite an Asian-American person from your school or area to compare and contrast living in his or her Asian homeland and the United States. Encourage children to ask questions and offer their own observations about possible similarities and differences. This information exchange should **provide students with current perceptions of and reactions to a culture different from their own**. To supplement the conversation, ask class members to fold a sheet of drawing paper into quarters and label the two top squares "alike," and the bottom squares, "different." Children may use one box to show American culture and one box to show Asian culture. For example, students might draw children attending school in both cultures in the "alike" boxes, and in the "different" boxes students might show different dining habits or beds.

ACTIVITY 3. To nurture the empathic dimension of citizenship, that is, appreciating various people and cultures, consider walking the class to a place where they will likely find many different kinds of people, including Asian-Americans, such as a museum, shopping center, cultural fair, or university. Teach them how to become participant-observers—researchers who join ongoing events while carefully noting the behaviors of those around them. Back in the classroom, help children reach conclusions about the what and why of the actions they have observed and guide them to the generalization that human behavior seems very diverse yet predictably constant.

Chapter 12

The Hispanic-American Experience—
Respecting a Culture
Past, Present, and Future

This chapter examines the citizenship experiences of Hispanic-Americans, whose roots lie in many different nations and whose influence has spanned many generations and will span many more to come. Young citizens can build important knowledge, abilities, and attitudes from the lessons these stories convey. The feature, alternate, and related titles allow learners of all ages, including teachers and librarians, to experience the rich and varied Hispanic-American heritage. These books foster mutual respect for perceived differences and encourage acceptance of known commonalities. Because the work so clearly advances our chapter vision, *Family Pictures/Cuadros de Familia* is our feature title. Our alternate and related titles elaborate this theme and expand teaching options.

Feature Title

Family Pictures/Cuadros de Familia by Carmen Lomas Garza. San Francisco: Children's Book Press, 1990. 30p. ISBN 0-892-39050-6.

In a series of 14 paintings, a Mexican-American artist shares fond memories of growing up in Texas. She details family traditions such as breaking piñatas at birthday parties and enacting Las Posadas. She chronicles everyday occurrences as well, such as picking oranges and swimming at Padre Island.

Lomas Garza's pictures and accompanying stories provide an excellent social studies resource, a feast of cultural detail that should increase awareness and empathy in younger students. The bilingual text adds to the book's teaching potential, particularly its capacity for initiating activities that build children's communication, decision-making, and interpersonal skills.

Alternate Titles

I Speak English for My Mom by Muriel Stanek. Illus. by Judith Friedman. Morton Grove, IL: A. Whitman, 1989. 32p. ISBN 0-807-53659-8.

The recently widowed Mrs. Gomez speaks only Spanish, so her daughter often must translate for her. In time, Lupe urges her mother to learn English. With her daughter's support and the prospect of finding a better job, Mrs. Gomez enrolls in an English class, expanding personal and occupational possibilities.

This story is an upbeat yet realistic addition to the literature of the Hispanic-American experience. Stanek portrays a strong mother-daughter relationship, focusing on Lupe's important role at home. The author clearly states Mrs. Gomez's willingness to sacrifice so she can reach a worthy goal—a model for young citizens everywhere. The book also introduces learning experiences that promote students' decision-making and social skills.

María Teresa by Mary Atkinson. Carrboro, NC: Lollipop Power, 1979. 39p. ISBN 0-914-99621-5.

> María Teresa Villaronga attends a new school after moving with her mother from New Mexico to Ohio. She gets discouraged when people are unfamiliar with the pronunciation of her name, have never heard of Masa Harina (a packaged tortilla dough mix), and rarely stock Spanish books in libraries. Her puppet, Monteja, finally helps her break the ice when she brings it to school one day. Because Monteja speaks only Spanish, her classmates insist on learning the language.

This book provides a solid lead-in to promote many competencies that young citizens need, like communicating, dealing with alternative viewpoints, solving problems, using maps and globes, and relating to others. Additionally, it supplies much information about Southwestern lifestyles and could spark many student research projects. Though sometimes difficult to locate, the book is well worth the effort to track it down.

Yagua Days by Cruz Martel. Illus. by Jerry Pinkney. New York: Dial Press, 1976. 40p. ISBN 0-803-79766-4.

> Adan, a young New Yorker, takes a surprise trip to his family's homeland, Puerto Rico, and discovers his amazingly diverse extended family. He also experiences his first round of "yagua days," those special times that are perfect for riding a palm frond down a long slope and into a waiting pool of water.

This older title can still contribute to children's understanding of Hispanic-American culture as exemplified in Puerto Rico. The author has provided a Spanish gazetteer that enhances students' understanding of what might be unfamiliar terminology. Martel's story also suggests chances for children to practice geographic and communication skills.

Related Titles

Abuela by Arthur Dorros. Illus. by Elisa Kleven. New York: Dutton Children's Books, 1991. 40p. ISBN 0-525-44750-4.

> When Rosalba visits the park with her *abuela* (grandmother), her fantasies inspire her to fly like the birds. In her imagination, Rosalba and Abuela soar over New York City.

Abuelita's Paradise by Carmen Santiago Nodar. Illus. by Diane Paterson. Morton Grove, IL: A. Whitman, 1992. 32p. ISBN 0-807-50129-8.

> Although her grandmother is dead, Marita sits in Abuelita's old rocking chair, remembering her tales of growing up in Puerto Rico.

The Adventures of Connie and Diego/Las aventuras de Connie y Diego by María García. Rev. ed. Trans. by Alma Flor Ada. Illus. by Malaquias Montoya. San Francisco: Children's Book Press, 1987. 24p. ISBN 0-892-39028-X.

In this English-Spanish story, Connie and Diego are born with multicolored skin in the Land of Plenty. They run away when people make fun of them. A tiger finally helps them achieve self-acceptance and learn the importance of expressing individuality while appreciating diversity.

Armando Asked, "Why?" by Jay Hulbert and Sid Kantor. Illus. by Pat Hoggan. Milwaukee, WI: Raintree, 1990. 24p. ISBN 0-817-23576-0.

Armando is an inquisitive boy, but he is frustrated when his family gets too busy to answer his questions. His problem is solved when his parents take him to the library. There, a helpful librarian provides books that satisfy his curiosity.

Aunt Elaine Does the Dance from Spain by Leah Komaiko. Illus. by Petra Mathers. New York: Doubleday, 1992. 32p. ISBN 0-385-30674-1.

In this humorous story, Aunt Elaine brings her niece to one of her performances. Katy watches in amazement as her aunt becomes another person, taking the stage and assuming the role of a Spanish dancer.

A Birthday Basket for Tía by Pat Mora. Illus. by Cecily Lang. New York: Macmillan, 1992. 32p. ISBN 0-027-67400-2.

This warm story recounts the preparations for Tía's 90th birthday party. As a special gift for her great-aunt, Cecelia puts together a basket of memories with loving care.

A Chicano Christmas Story/Un Cuento Navideño Chicano by Manuel Cruz and Ruth Cruz. Illus. by Manuel Cruz. Los Angeles: Bilingual Educational Services, 1981. 48p. ISBN 0-86624-000-4 (paper).

A family experiences difficult times in this English-Spanish story. Elenita's and Diego's father has been laid off from several jobs. Fortunately, hardworking community members share life's necessities with those less fortunate.

Con Mi Hermano/With My Brother by Eileen Roe. Illus. by Robert Casilla. New York: Bradbury Press, 1991. 32p. ISBN 0-027-77373-6.

Roe's bilingual text depicts how a young boy admires his older brother and wants to be just like him.

The Farolitos of Christmas: A New Mexican Christmas Story by Rudolfo Anaya. Illus. by Richard C. Sandoval. Santa Fe, NM: New Mexico Magazine, 1987. 32p. ISBN 0-937-20606-7.

Anaya's story offers an explanation for the popular holiday practice of *luminarias,* or *farolitos.* Three days before Christmas, Luz, a fourth-grade girl, lights votive candles and places them in sand-filled paper bags outside her home.

Friends from the Other Side/Amigos del Otro Lado by Gloria Anzaldua. Illus. by Consuelo Mendez. San Francisco: Children's Book Press, 1993. 32p. ISBN 0-89239-113-8.

Joaquin and his mother have recently crossed the Rio Grande into Texas, searching for a new life. As troubles mount, they receive help from Prietita, a brave Mexican-American girl.

Gilberto and the Wind by Marie Hall Ets. New York: Viking, 1963. 32p. ISBN 0-670-34025-1 (paper).

This older, impressionistic work portrays Gilberto and the wind playing tag with one another.

Hello, Amigos! by Tricia Brown. Photos by Fran Ortiz. New York: Henry Holt, 1986. 48p. ISBN 0-805-00090-9.

Frankie Valdez, a Mexican-American boy living in San Francisco, outlines happenings on a most special day—his birthday.

How Many Days to America? A Thanksgiving Story by Eve Bunting. Illus. by Beth Peck. New York: Clarion Books, 1988. 32p. ISBN 0-899-19521-0.

A family leaves an unnamed Caribbean island "the night the soldiers came." Reaching the U.S. coast, the refugees learn that they have arrived on an especially appropriate holiday, Thanksgiving.

Mr. Sugar Came to Town/La Visita del Señor Azúcar, adapted by Harriet Rohmer and Cruz Gómez. Trans. by Rosalma Zubizarreta. Illus. by Enrique Chagoya. San Francisco: Children's Book Press, 1989. 32p. ISBN 0-892-39045-X.

Rohmer and Gómez adapted this story from a puppet play produced by the Food and Nutrition Program of the Watsonville, California Rural Health Clinic. Mr. Sugar's truck of sweets tempts Alicia and Alfredo. Fortunately, Grandma Lupe unmasks Mr. Sugar and the children regain their senses.

My Best Friend, Martha Rodríguez: Meeting a Mexican-American Family by Dianne MacMillan and Dorothy Freeman. Illus. by Warren Fricke. Englewood Cliffs, NJ: Messner, 1986. 48p. ISBN 0-671-61973-X.

Kathy's friendship with Martha and her family introduces her to their culture's social life, customs, songs, and games.

My Mother and I Are Growing Strong/Mi Mama y Yo Nos Hacemos Fuerte by Inez Maury. Trans. by Anna Muñoz. Illus. by Sandy Speidel. Berkeley, CA: New Seed Press, 1979. 28p. ISBN 0-938-67806-X.

Emilita and her mother, Lupe, tend Mr. Stubblebine's garden, working father's job while he is in prison. Soon to be released, he will find two stronger females, two who can do "men's work" when he returns home.

My Mother, the Mail Carrier/Mi Mama la Cartera by Inez Maury. Trans. by Norah Alemany. Illus. by Lady McCrady. New York: Feminist Press, 1976. 29p. ISBN 0-935-31223-4.

Lupita's mother, Mariana, a mail carrier, is strong, kind, and wise, as well as a good cook, but Lupita does not wish to follow in her footsteps. Instead, she hopes to become a jockey.

Pancho's Piñata by Stefan Czernecki and Timothy Rhodes. Illus. by Stefan Czernecki. New York: Hyperion, 1992. 40p. ISBN 1-562-82277-2.

Inspired by Diego Rivera's mural *La Piñata and Procession,* the authors retell the tale of Pancho's mystical adventure that brought the piñata into Hispanic tradition.

Rosita's Christmas Wish by Mary Ann Smothers Bruni. Illus. by Thom Ricks. San Antonio, TX: Texart, 1985. 48p. ISBN 0-935-85700-1.

Through nine-year-old Rosita's eyes, readers glimpse customs, family life, celebrations, and special foods and take a closer look at the traditional Christmas drama *Pastorela* (Shepherds' Play).

Treasure Nap by Juanita Havill. Illus. by Elivia Savadier. Boston: Houghton Mifflin, 1992. 32p. ISBN 0-3955-7817-5.

One hot afternoon, a young girl asks her mother to relate the story of the journey great-great-grandmother made from Mexico to the United States, carrying her treasures: a serape (blanket), a pito (flute), and a wooden bird cage.

Teaching Options

Family Pictures/Cuadros de Familia or any of the alternate and related titles supply characters, setting, and content for the following activities. As in past chapters, activities rarely rely on specific titles but may be more meaningful with some books than with others. These teaching ideas should be modified as necessary and might yield richer results if introduced by several story selections.

Like other portions of section 4, this chapter may include stories that hit close to home and prove troubling for some students, depending on their backgrounds and experiences. *María Teresa,* for example, treats a child's sense of alienation in fairly direct terms. In *My Mother and I Are Growing Strong/Mi Mama y Yo Nos Hacemos Fuerte,* mother and daughter keep bodies and souls together while father serves time in prison. No teacher can predict which child will react emotionally to a read-aloud selection. At the same time, a brief chat with a particular student before or after a potentially disturbing story might maximize learning for all students in your class.

Activities of the Head: Building Citizenship Understandings

ACTIVITY 1. In this activity, children start the process of **learning a language, an important step in fostering cultural appreciation**. Children often acquire bits and pieces of a second language quickly, as they enjoy repeating basic words and numbers. Because many titles cited in this chapter are bilingual, students and teacher have an opportunity to compare and contrast the vocabularies and grammars of the two languages.

After reading these books aloud, display them in the classroom and encourage children to examine them at their leisure, finding words that look alike, establishing usage patterns, and deciding which words match others. Enlist a Spanish-speaking teacher, parent, or older student as a resource person. Periodically conduct a whole-class dialogue in which children note the similarities between Spanish and English, especially the number of words that transfer directly from one language to the other.

ACTIVITY 2. This activity allows children to **proceed along another path toward appreciating an ethnic heritage—exploring holiday customs and traditions**. Although many celebrations appear in this chapter's book selections, most titles feature Hispanic-American Christmas traditions (e.g., *Family Pictures*, *A Chicano Christmas Story*, *Rosita's Christmas Wish*, *The Farolitos of Christmas*, and *My Best Friend, Martha Rodríquez*). Read one or more of these stories aloud, then encourage students to highlight interesting and unusual Christmas customs, comparing and contrasting them with practices that their own families observe. At an appropriate season, help children select several appealing Hispanic holiday traditions, field-test them in the classroom, and enjoy them with family members.

To extend the activity, include customs from other cultures, such as Asian-American, African-American, and Native American, in the class discussion and try out these observances as well. To **foster geographic skills**, children can mark the origin of each holiday tradition on a world map or globe.

ACTIVITY 3. This activity should help children **acknowledge the strong Hispanic influence on American music, dance, and the visual arts**. Several titles provide introductory information about the impact of Hispanic artists. To inspire children to investigate further, share any of the following books: *My Best Friend, Martha Rodríguez*; *A Birthday Basket for Tía*; *Aunt Elaine Does the Dance from Spain*; *Hello, Amigos!*; *Rosita's Christmas Wish*; or *Family Pictures*. To focus their research, consider steering children to research the creative efforts of Mexican and Mexican-American artists. At the same time, students' backgrounds and community demographics may dictate a wider, more inclusive investigation. Whatever its scope, make the inquiry a collaborative project. Let children, parents, community leaders, classroom teachers, media specialists, librarians, and music teachers discover abundant songs, dances, paintings, sculptures, architectural designs, and photographs for primary children to share with classmates and other students.

Activities of the Hand: Building Citizenship Skills

ACTIVITY 1. Several titles reference Spanish-speaking countries and regions, suggesting opportunities to **promote children's map and globe skills and geographic understanding, as well as their reference skills and ability to process information**. When read and discussed, these books acquaint students with basic information about the locations, climates, lifestyles, and economic systems of Hispanic areas, including Puerto Rico (*Yagua Days* and *Abuelita's Paradise*); Mexico (*Family Pictures*, *A Chicano Christmas Story*, *Treasure Nap*, and *My Best Friend, Martha Rodríguez*); and the Caribbean (*How Many Days to America?*). Additionally, these stories might prompt students to locate these settings on a regional map or a globe; to investigate them further using trade books and basic reference tools, with assistance as necessary; and to communicate findings to classmates in creative ways, such as drawings, booklets, or a television talk show.

Needless to say, there are many other places around the world where Spanish is the primary language. Older primary children could use media center resources to uncover the names and locations of additional Spanish-speaking countries. Let students locate as many places as possible and mark them on maps or globes or both. For children with strong reading skills, enrich the activity further by providing current world population figures; having students break the numbers down by language spoken; and helping them draw conclusions regarding the relative global influences of Spanish, English, Chinese, and other languages.

ACTIVITY 2. In this quick follow-up to the previous activity, **students build geographic skills while investigating a concept (island) that often appears on lists of social studies essentials for the primary grades**. Read and review *Yagua Days*, or *Abuelita's Paradise*, or both, then group students into pairs or trios and have them locate Puerto Rico on maps of various types (e.g., topographical, political, regional, world). Let them compare and contrast their findings, establishing the common features of the maps that they have consulted. Continue the dialogue by writing the term *island*, on the chalkboard or overhead. Consider what makes Puerto Rico an island, and determine the essential attributes that every island must display.

To extend the activity, have small groups of older primary students make topographical maps of Puerto Rico from salt and flour, clay, or some other readily available material.

ACTIVITY 3. The piñata, a well-known symbol of Hispanic culture, invites children to join the festivities, **boosting their social participation skills in the process**. Two stories can introduce the activity: *My Best Friend, Martha Rodríguez* (the Anglo main character models the excitement that the piñata can produce) and *Pancho's Piñata* (the author traces the custom's background, noting that the practice may have origins in China and Italy as well as Spain and Mexico).

After a read-and-discuss session, encourage students to make piñatas by covering inflated balloons with papier-mâché strips. Have children work in small groups; when they finish, take time to debrief about social behaviors that facilitated group efforts and increased productivity (e.g., cooperation, open communication, positive comments, listening to each other). To add an intriguing twist to the activity, hold the piñata celebration in conjunction with a relatively obscure holiday, such as Arbor Day or Groundhog Day, rather than during the Christmas season, when the tradition is typically observed.

Activities of the Heart: Building Citizenship Dispositions

ACTIVITY 1. Translating from native to foreign language can befuddle and distress most people. **Help students identify with individuals who must communicate in a new language** by having them complete this activity. Browse through the bilingual titles cited in this chapter to remind children that, while many languages share similar words, a daunting number of terms are unique to a particular language. Ask children if they know anyone who is learning English as a second language. Invite this guest speaker to share how the task of translating back and forth between two languages makes him or her feel. To conclude the activity, serve as the facilitator as students brainstorm ways to assist and support schoolmates who must learn bilingually. Appoint a committee to record these suggestions and post them in a visible location.

Fig. 12. A list of student recommendations. *(Written by Rodrigo Cedillo, age 8; ideas by Mitchell Schick, age 8, and Rodrigo Cedillo)*

ACTIVITY 2. Although students should familiarize themselves with other cultures, they should also **discover more about their own cultural backgrounds, raising their sense of pride in their heritage**. As you read aloud selected titles, affirm children's recognition of the term *cultural identity*, and their grasp of its implications. Remember that children need not define cultural identity in technical terms; they should just be able to give a sense of what the phrase means to them or provide examples of the term in action.

Then ask each child to think of important traditions, songs, games, and stories that are part of her or his background. Form small groups and let children converse about these experiences with classmates representing a cross-section of the neighborhood. In the sharing process, nurture appreciative, supportive comments and guide students to acknowledge the value of keeping an open mind and heart.

To extend the activity, allow children to carry this cultural exchange beyond classroom walls. Organize sharing groups across classrooms and grade levels. Arrange for students to write pen pals at other schools in your community or even in different states or regions.

ACTIVITY 3. This activity **promotes students' ability to recognize and emulate constructive, cooperative approaches to problem solving and decision making.** Hispanic-American characters in several stories model citizenship traits that today's children might well observe in action. In *I Speak English for My Mom, A Chicano Christmas Story, Mr. Sugar Came to Town, María Teresa,* and *How Many Days to America?*, Hispanic citizens resolve pressing personal difficulties with the assistance of family members, friends, and community leaders. As children listen to these stories and discuss their meanings, help them comprehend that tackling problems cooperatively and practicing decision making by consensus typify the Hispanic culture. So children can grasp that cooperative methods can yield positive results for anyone, help them compare and contrast the approaches used by Hispanic-American characters with techniques demonstrated by representatives of different cultures. Consult stories listed in the other chapters in section 4 to find examples for comparison.

Chapter 13

The Native American Experience— Hearing Powerful Stories

Our final chapter advances stories and activities that enlighten young readers about the experiences of Native Americans from many tribes and nations. They have lived with this land for countless centuries. Their past and present blessings have been mixed, comprised of joy and sorrow, victory and defeat. Children should recognize the contributions that native peoples have made to our way of life and the changes that have been forced on their cultures. As they encounter this chapter's literature selections, youngsters should increase their awareness of the Native American legacy as they develop social studies skills and take actions that reflect a sense of civic responsibility. Because of its acclaimed accuracy and subtle humor, we have chosen *Who-Paddled-Backward-With-Trout* as our feature title. We include alternate and related titles that also tell powerful stories and suggest potentially potent teaching ideas.

Feature Title

Who-Paddled-Backward-With-Trout by Howard Norman. Illus. by Ed Young. Boston: Little, Brown, 1987. 32p. ISBN 0-316-61182-4.

As told to the author by an 82-year-old Canadian Indian, a young Cree boy, Trout-With-Flattened-Nose, dislikes his name so intensely that he embarks on a quest to find a new one. His father supports the unusual mission but warns his son that he cannot just pick a name, he must earn it. Through a series of comical misadventures, the boy identifies and acquires a name that makes him proud.

Native American critics have praised Norman's retold story for its authenticity. Besides relating appropriate cultural information, the story suggests various teaching options that explore important social studies themes like respecting one's cultural heritage and working hard to achieve worthy goals. These activities might also promote vital citizenship competencies such as the skills of problem solving, decision making, and communication.

Alternate Titles

Ashkii and His Grandfather by Margaret Kahn Garaway. Illus. by Harry Warren. Tucson, AZ: Treasure Chest Publications, 1989. 33p. ISBN 0-918-08041-X.

Ashkii spends his sixth summer with his grandfather, tending sheep and learning to draw. Ashkii does not want to leave camp to start kindergarten and runs away from school shortly after his first day in the classroom. Drawing from the wisdom of the old ways, his grandfather helps the boy realize that he must practice the school's new ways to achieve his dream—becoming a Navajo artist.

Garaway reinforces the value of preserving strong, intergenerational family ties, as well as other dispositions that can guide young citizens, such as the value of education and the need for civic responsibility. Her story can also help young readers develop skills necessary for active citizenship, such as social participation, inquiry, and decision making.

An Eskimo Birthday by Tom D. Robinson. Illus. by Glo Coalson. New York: Dodd, Mead, 1975. 40p. ISBN 0-396-07065-5.

On her birthday, Eeka expresses her fondest wish, acquiring enough furs to finish her new parka. In telling Eeka's simple story, the author interjects considerable information about Alaska's old and new ways of life.

Some aspects of this sensitive story seem a bit dated. For example, Robinson references the native people as Eskimo rather than Inuit. Still, the book contributes much usable information to studies of Native American lifestyles and promotes students' communication skills. The work also adds an affective dimension to any social studies program, conveying and reinforcing themes that underlie productive citizenship teaching in the primary grades (e.g., cross-cultural understanding, empathy with others, respect for differences).

The Goat in the Rug by Geraldine, as told to Charles L. Blood and Martin Link. Illus. by Nancy Winslow Parker. Reprint of 1976 ed. New York: Macmillan, 1984. 40p. ISBN 0-027-10920-8.

Blood and Martin craft a wonderfully amusing tale that sneaks up on young readers with great quantities of useful and accurate information. In an apparently exclusive "interview," Geraldine the Goat recounts the steps that her Navajo friend Glenmae must follow to make an authentic Navajo rug.

This clever story supports primary social studies teaching in many ways. The work supplies accurate details about Navajo rug making while nurturing a deeper understanding of a Native American approach to life. Human and animal characters apply citizenship skills in real-life settings, cooperating effectively to avert a near-disaster, making social decisions repeatedly, and critically thinking through problems as they arise. They also model citizenship dispositions, particularly the commitment to stick with a project until a worthy goal is achieved.

Related Titles

Ahyoka and the Talking Leaves by Peter Roop and Connie Roop. Illus. by Yoshi Miyake. New York: Lothrop, Lee & Shepard, 1992. 60p. ISBN 0-688-10697-8.

In a traditional story based on an actual event, a young girl helps her father unlock the secret of the "talking leaves" (the letters and books from which the white man gains knowledge). With Ahyoka's assistance, Sequoyah develops an alphabet for the Cherokee people.

Antelope Woman: An Apache Folktale, retold and illus. by Michael Lacapa. Flagstaff, AZ: Northland, 1992. 48p. ISBN 0-873-58543-7.

As he tells the tale of Antelope Woman, a tribal elder convinces a young man that the Apache must honor all living things, whether great or small.

A Boy Becomes a Man at Wounded Knee by Ted Wood with Wanbli Numpa Afraid of Hawk. New York: Walker, 1992. 42p. ISBN 0-802-78175-6.

This nonfiction book recounts a symbolic effort to mend the damage left by the Wounded Knee Massacre of 1890. Wanbli Numpa Afraid of Hawk, an Oglala Lakota, describes the ride taken with his father, grandfather, and other tribal members to commemorate the tragedy's centennial year.

Death of the Iron Horse by Paul Goble. New York: Bradbury Press, 1987. 32p. ISBN 0-027-37830-6.

From the Cheyenne people's perspective, Goble depicts an 1867 incident in the Indian Wars, the intentional wreck of a Union Pacific train.

Dragonfly's Tale retold and illus. by Kristina Rodanas. New York: Clarion Books, 1991. 32p. ISBN 0-395-57003-4.

Years ago, according to a Zuni tale, the Ashiwi offended the Corn Maidens by wasting a bountiful harvest. A brother and sister regain the maidens' goodwill with the help of a toy dragonfly made from cornstalks.

Dreamcatcher by Audrey Osofsky. Illus. by Ed Young. New York: Orchard Books, 1992. 32p. ISBN 0-531-08588-0.

Long ago in the land of the Ojibwa, a baby sleeps serenely, while the tribe proceeds with everyday activities, confident that a "dreamcatcher" will protect the infant from nightmares.

The Girl Who Loved Wild Horses by Paul Goble. New York: Bradbury Press, 1982. 32p. ISBN 0-027-36570-0.

Vivid illustrations and straightforward text have raised this book to near-classic status. Goble touches young readers with the story of an Indian girl who so loves wandering with a herd of wild horses that she finally becomes one.

The Great Change by White Deer of Autumn. Illus. by Carol Grigg. Hillsboro, OR: Beyond Words, 1992. ISBN 0-941-83179-5.

When nine-year-old Wanba asks why her grandfather had to die, her grand-mother struggles to find the right way to explain the "Great Change" to a child.

The Legend of the Bluebonnet: An Old Tale of Texas, retold and illus. by Tomie dePaola. New York: Putnam, 1983. 30p. ISBN 0-399-20937-9.

DePaola retells the Comanche folktale in which a young girl's sacrifice brings the bluebonnet, a delicate flower, to Texas.

The Legend of the Indian Paintbrush, retold and illus. by Tomie dePaola. New York: Putnam, 1988. 40p. ISBN 0-399-21534-4.

A dream-vision implies that Little Gopher, a Plains Indian, will become an artist. The prediction rings true when the boy transports the colors of the sunset from sky to earth.

Mama, Do You Love Me? by Barbara M. Joosse. Illus. by Barbara Lavallee. San Francisco: Chronicle Books, 1991. ISBN 0-877-01759-X.

In northern Alaska long ago, an Inuit girl asks about her mother's love. The child tests her mother with hypothetical situations, but the woman responds that she will always love her daughter, no matter how angry she may get.

Moonsong Lullaby by Jamake Highwater. Photos by Marcia Keegan. New York: Lothrop, Lee & Shepard, 1981. 32p. ISBN 0-688-00427-X.

This gentle poem explains aspects of Native American culture in terms of night life in the woods. Although several animals appear in improper settings, the tone of this work makes it a viable resource.

The Mud Pony: A Traditional Skidi Pawnee Tale retold by Caron Lee Cohen. Illus. by Shonto Begay. New York: Scholastic, 1988. 32p. ISBN 0-590-41525-5.

A poor boy rises to tribal leadership, validating the Pawnee belief that one of humble origin can achieve great things. Mother Earth assists the youngster by transforming his mud pony into a real one; the spirit then forces him to find his own strength by returning the horse to mud.

My Grandmother's Cookie Jar by Montzalee Miller. Illus. by Katherine Potter. Los Angeles: Price Stern Sloan, 1987. 30p. ISBN 0-843-11587-4.

Each time a girl eats a treat from her grandmother's cookie jar, she hears a tale about her ancestors. When her grandmother dies, the girl promises her grandfather that she will keep the stories alive.

Not Just Any Ring by Danita Haller. Illus. by Deborah Kogan Ray. New York: Alfred A. Knopf, 1982. 48p. ISBN 0-394-95082-8.

Through her grandfather's wisdom, a small child understands that good fortune lies within her heart, not in a good-luck ring.

On Mother's Lap by Ann H. Scott. Illus. by Glo Coalson. Rev. ed. New York: Clarion Books, 1992. 32p. ISBN 0-395-58920-7.

Scott's story emphasizes that a mother's love transcends cultural boundaries; her lap has room for everything and everyone, including Michael, an Inuit boy, and his baby sister.

The Secret of the Seal by Deborah Davis. Illus. by Judy Labrasca. New York: Crown, 1989. 57p. ISBN 0-517-56725-3.

Kyo, an Inuit boy, intends to kill his first seal but makes friends with his prey instead, naming it Tooky. In a believable way, the boy shifts from hunter to conservationist in this story for older primary children.

Sky Dogs by Jane Yolen. Illus. by Barry Moser. San Diego, CA: Harcourt Brace Jovanovich, 1990. 32p. ISBN 0-152-75480-6.

The author combines several stories to create this fable told by He-Who-Loves-Horses, who explains how the horse came to the Blackfeet.

Thirteen Moons on Turtle's Back: A Native American Year of Moons by Joseph Bruchac and Jonathan London. Illus. by Thomas Locker. New York: Philomel, 1992. 32p. ISBN 0-399-22141-7.

In this poetry anthology, Bruchac and London collect Native American legends, folktales, and stories illustrating nature's progress through the seasons.

Very Last First Time by Jan Andrews. Illus. by Ian Wallace. New York: Atheneum, 1986. 32p. ISBN 0-689-50388-1.

Andrews allows children to experience an Inuit girl's emotions as she gathers mussels and explores the world that lies between the sea bottom and the frozen ice.

Teaching Options

Introduce one or more of the following teaching ideas after reading and discussing any of the feature, alternate, or related titles. We rarely focused on a single book as we developed a learning experience, although some activities may proceed more effectively with particular stories. Please modify our suggestions as your children's knowledge and ability levels dictate. As always, include several books in an activity whenever possible to create compare-and-contrast opportunities for children.

Additionally, our chapter theme involves Native American cultural groups whose recent past has proven difficult, even tragic, and whose present often seems accompanied by controversy. Native American societies, moreover, were not literate in our modern sense, relying on oral and pictorial traditions that lose much in the translation to printed text. As a result, you can rarely determine what understandings children will take from a story, and seldom predict what emotional reactions a book might occasion for children. Supply yourself with as much background information about a story's setting, plot, and characters as you possibly can. And be prepared to counsel and support students who seem distressed by an author's treatment of a sensitive topic or theme.

Activities of the Head: Building Citizenship Understandings

ACTIVITY 1. A name holds great power for the person who owns it. Many Native American cultures, in fact, conceived relatively elaborate rituals for name giving. Several titles highlight how names are bestowed, including *Who-Paddled-Backward-With-Trout*, *Sky Dogs*, *The Girl Who Loved Wild Horses*, and *The Legend of the Bluebonnet*.

After reading any or all of these titles aloud, introduce this activity so **students can gain understanding about the power of names, rationales for name giving, and the nature of naming ceremonies.** As you share your selections, note that Indian tribes have bestowed names in various ways and for many reasons. Ask students to recall the names mentioned in the stories, writing each one on the chalkboard, overhead, or on a sheet of butcher paper. Review why these names were chosen, why they were changed in several instances, and how they were bestowed on their owners. Help children speculate about the ways in which names influenced the lives of story characters.

Then assist each student as he or she examines reference materials in the media center to locate the meaning of his or her name. For an engaging homework assignment, have children discuss their names with parents or the significant adult or adults at home. Students can complete the activity by writing brief explanations, with accompanying illustrations, summarizing the meanings that their names were intended to convey.

ACTIVITY 2. From an early age, children are aware of living creatures. By the time they enter school, students might even grasp the significant role that animals play in the lifestyles and customs of most societies. This activity **fosters understanding of the contributions that mammals, fish, birds, and insects have made to Native American lifestyles and the spiritual meanings that these creatures carry.** First, read as many titles as possible, because almost all of them refer to material and spiritual relevance that living things hold for various tribal groups. Working in pairs or trios, children can identify the animals that are mentioned in particular stories and brainstorm the manner in which they are treated by Native American characters. To help students determine how tribes use and portray different creatures, small groups should classify the results of their brainstorming, for example, animals used for transportation; animals that provide clothing, food, or shelter; and legendary animals revered in religious ceremony. Provide time for children to examine and draw conclusions from these categories.

For enrichment, older primary children can illustrate the special relationship between Native American cultures and living things using a variety of artistic media. Students might also compare and contrast this relationship with other ways that our society treats animals. Additionally, they might consult reference materials or guest experts or both to learn the names for selected creatures in various Native American languages, then share these terms with classmates.

ACTIVITY 3. Most titles mentioned in this chapter show different types of Indian dwellings (e.g., *Ashkii and His Grandfather*, *The Goat in the Rug*, *An Eskimo Birthday*, *Sky Dogs*, *Dreamcatcher*). **To encourage children to analyze the functions of Native American homes, whatever form they may take,** read aloud as many relevant titles as time allows. Concurrently, ask students to read additional stories individually or in small groups, paying particular attention to the shelters depicted in each. Have them examine the shapes and functions of the various houses they encounter. Then direct each small group to study one type of home, focusing on the ways in which it meets the needs and satisfies the wants of the family living in it. To share information, each group can contribute a section of a "Native American Dwellings" mural and explain this artwork to classmates. Groups might also construct models of Indian dwellings like hogans, tepees, and igloos, and analyze the forms and functions of these homes in a class conversation.

Activities of the Hand: Building Citizenship Skills

ACTIVITY 1. While completing activities presented in chapter 11, students learned how Asian cultures communicate with written symbols or characters. In a general sense, activity 1 **reinforces children's understanding that different cultures transmit information through various forms of written language, while building their communication skills**. More specifically, the experience **provides an opportunity to research and design examples of Native American pictographic art**.

Begin by reading and discussing *Ashkii and His Grandfather, The Goat in the Rug, Ahyoka and the Talking Leaves,* or all three. Focus conversation on the instances of pictographic communications that these books contain. Ensure that children grasp the essential attributes of a pictograph (e.g., a picture drawn or painted to convey ideas or objects or both). Then select a small group of students, send them to the media center to find further examples of pictographs, and let them report their findings. If possible, invite an expert to explain these symbols or visit a site where pictographic writing has been preserved. Prepare a handout with simple pictographic messages and allow children, working in pairs or trios, to decode them.

To culminate the experience, ask pairs of children to create pictographs that convey meaning from one story character to another (e.g., Ashkii to his grandfather; Glenmae to Geraldine; Ahyoka to her father, Sequoyah). Then have each pair role-play its pictograph while classmates try to decipher its meaning. Let students dialogue about the relative effectiveness of pictographic communication to conclude the activity.

ACTIVITY 2. To boost communication skills further and add emphasis to children's understanding of Indian pictographs, read aloud stories featuring a Plains setting (e.g., *The Mud Pony, Sky Dogs, The Girl Who Loved Wild Horses, Death of the Iron Horse*). Focus discussion on the modes of communication featured in these tales. As the opportunity arises, introduce the term *winter count* and explain that every winter, members of the Plains tribes depicted a significant happening from the past year on a buffalo hide, accumulating a record of events much as people might keep a lifelong journal. Indicate that this story of the past usually started in the center of the skin, spiraling outward to the edges.

As an engaging art project, allow each child to create his or her own winter count, done in the tradition of the Plains Indians, recording significant events from the past year. Should a year prove too lengthy a time frame, let students picture happenings from the previous month or week. Remind students that each pictograph records a memorable happening; the first should be drawn at the center of the hide. Strive for authenticity, but if tanned skins are unavailable, substitute pieces of leather or brown paper bags that have been torn to shape, then waxed. Provide time for children to share their projects and display them on a wall or bulletin board.

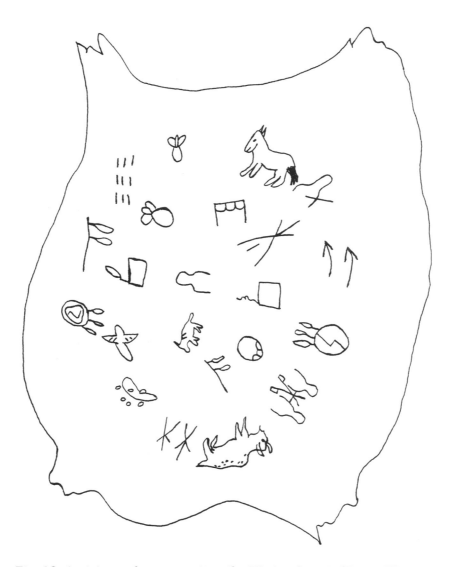

Fig. 13. A pictograph representing the Winter Count. *(Vivian Winter Chaser, teacher)*

ACTIVITY 3. Dreams play a part in several titles, suggesting this opportunity to **promote students' information-processing skills and ability to follow directions**. After reading *The Legend of the Indian Paintbrush, The Mud Pony,* or *Dreamcatcher,* let students dialogue about the ways that story characters interpreted their dreams (e.g., as glimpses of the future, as practical advice, as bad omens or nightmares). Revisit the passages from *Dreamcatcher* in which Big Sister crafts an artwork that captures "dark dreams" while permitting "good dreams" to drift through and visit a sleeping infant. Once interest in the dreamcatcher has been kindled, delegate small groups of students to find additional information about these mystical charms, as well as illustrations of dreamcatchers and directions for making them. Better yet, invite a Native American artist who could demonstrate how to craft one. If possible, allow students to follow these instructions, making dreamcatchers and sharing their creations with classmates.

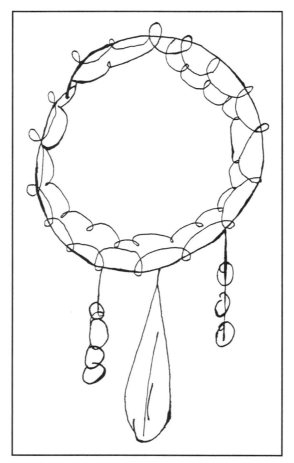

Fig. 14. A design for a dreamcatcher.
(Vivian Winter Chaser, teacher)

ACTIVITY 4. This activity **builds information-processing and critical-thinking skills** as children study the role of the visual arts in Native American cultures. As you read *The Girl Who Loved Wild Horses, The Goat in the Rug, The Legend of the Indian Paintbrush,* or all three, ask students to note which paint and dye colors were used in various forms of illustration and the sources for each hue (e.g., soils, crushed flowers, boiled roots). Discuss these observations, guiding students to conclude that these colors typically represented themes or values.

Then let small groups of children create a chart showing the colors frequently selected by Native American artists, the meaning that each shade conveyed, and possible sources for each hue. Young people might also classify Native American illustrations by their meaning or function (e.g., practical, decorative, religious, symbolic). Finally, have each student create one of these types of drawings with water-soluble paints and dyes, using colors that a Native American artist might have chosen.

Activities of the Heart: Building Citizenship Dispositions

ACTIVITY 1. Young citizens should **develop and demonstrate empathy for all people, especially their elders.** Read and discuss *My Grandmother's Cookie Jar, Not Just Any Ring, The Great Change, Eskimo Birthday, Ashkii and His Grandfather,* or *A Boy Becomes a Man at Wounded Knee* to introduce the activity. Then ask students to recall how the young showed reverence and respect toward the old in these stories. Encourage children to specify what young and old characters did together. For example, they baked cookies and told stories to solve problems, to build strength of character, or to express their love. They tended the sheep, drew pictures, and reminisced about the past. Have children brainstorm constructive and fun things to do with grandparents and older friends.

To conclude the activity, have each student invite a grandparent or older friend to visit the classroom (have backups ready should guests be unable to attend). Let each youngster share a favorite story with her or his guest, then have a class representative read the list of things that youngsters and oldsters might try together. Finally, provide enough supplies that each pair might try at least one fun thing to do and enough time for sharing reactions to the experience in a class conversation.

ACTIVITY 2. Many Native American people understand and respect life cycles, as indicated in many selections. For example, *The Goat in the Rug* shows the progression from goat to wool to blanket. *The Great Change* and *My Grandmother's Cookie Jar* depict a reverence for the aging process and a recognition of the naturalness of death. *Thirteen Moons on Turtle's Back* traces the moon's monthly phases. This activity **fosters students' appreciation for the number and meaning of cycles found in nature and for the importance that these cycles have held for Native American cultures.**

As you read one or more of these stories, encourage students to consider the life cycle as well as other natural sequences that parallel the four seasons. Guide them to the recognition that Native American legends and stories often unfold events in cyclical patterns. To represent their new understandings visually, children could create a series of four posters that demonstrate the yearly growth cycle—its beginning in the spring, development in summer, maturity in autumn, and waning in winter. Encourage them to adopt Native American forms and styles in their artwork. After displaying the posters, nurture quiet conversation about the nature of the life cycle and support children as they express their feelings about the consequences that this pattern inevitably must produce.

ACTIVITY 3. Young citizens acquire great quantities of Head and Hand as they travel in the outdoors (e.g., learning about their surroundings, studying maps, plotting directions). At the same time, an orienteering activity can also **stimulate considerable amounts of Heart, particularly a feel for the intuitive, sensitive modes of traveling that Native Americans typically practiced**. The activity should also **promote students' geographic and decision-making skills**. *The Very Last First Time* and *Moonsong Lullaby* can serve as wonderful vehicles for achieving these instructional purposes.

After sharing these two books, present information about the ways in which Native Americans determined direction and relative location. For example, they could discern not only the direction traveled but the amount of time elapsed since animals passed by, after examining the prints and markings that these creatures left. Indians marked trails and identified "decision points" with twisted grasses, bent twigs, and rock piles. They sighted stars, sun, and moon to establish direction while traveling. Invite a guest expert like a pilot, a scout leader, or a military officer to inform children about other ways that travelers consult natural phenomena to find their way.

Ph.7. Children orienteering on playground. *(Gary Brian, Joseph Smith, Tyler Okluvich)*

So young citizens can apply and appreciate their new knowledge, let small groups try intuitive, natural methods to guide themselves around the playground. After some practice, allow them to navigate around the school neighborhood. Once children become true pathfinders, have them demonstrate their closeness with nature by leading schoolmates and parents on short journeys of exploration.

Epilogue

Originally, we anticipated that our work would be complete after presenting roughly 200 story selections and over 125 activities introduced by these titles. We imagined sharing these teaching resources, then riding into the sunset with readers speculating, "Who were those masked authors?" But as we readied these 13 chapters for publication, we realized that some loose ends remained. Who should use these teaching ideas? How can they be implemented most effectively? How should these learning experiences be incorporated in the primary curriculum? Our concluding remarks answer these questions, and, we hope, encourage primary teachers to expand their use of literature-based teaching beyond our recommended books and activities.

Who Should Use These Teaching Resources?

The response to this question seems automatic—social studies teachers, of course! After all, appreciating diversity seems a requirement for informed citizenship; promoting civic competence is the stated mission for social studies educators. In reality, the answer is not that simple. As primary teachers know so well, young children acquire citizenship knowledge, skills, and dispositions throughout the school day. Civic education is an ongoing process in the early grades, rarely confined to social studies classes. Young citizens will not learn to appreciate diversity through discrete lessons lasting 45 minutes each.

Teachers of every subject area nurture young citizens' appreciation of our differences and commonalities. The entire support staff—librarians, special educators, and administrators as well as aides, secretaries, cooks, and custodians—is involved in civic education as well. Public librarians, youth leaders, parents, curriculum coordinators, and lesson designers also assume some responsibility for fostering appreciative citizenship. In short, everyone who actively promotes the civic competence of young children might utilize these books and activities to extend and enrich their repertoires of learning experiences.

Although targeting many types of citizenship teachers, we must admit that literature-based instruction is neither the traditional nor the easy way to proceed. Quite frankly, integrated, literature-based learning experiences can get messy. Even primary students will question the status quo; they will move around; they will even converse with one another! Children might seem confused when the teacher does not deliver right answers. Picture books and storybooks, moreover, do not outline lesson plans or specify behavioral objectives. Works of fiction may not correlate closely with items on standardized tests. Our ideas chart a direction and provide a starting point. The teacher may have miles to go before our suggestions become classroom practice.

In summary, we crafted this activity book for those concerned citizens who help young children gain and exercise appreciative citizenship. These educators, librarians, parents, and community leaders share our belief that primary students can only become citizens by acting like citizens. Our teaching ideas engage students, prompting them to think, encouraging them to feel, and inviting them to take civic action. Quite possibly, these activities can influence citizenship teachers in similar ways. As they read aloud our story selections and implement the accompanying activities, adults will model the reflection, empathy, sense of commitment, and, yes, even the risk taking that young citizens should emulate.

How Can These Teaching Ideas Be Implemented Most Effectively?

As we have suggested, helping young children appreciate diversity through literature involves some risk. You can maximize chances for success by noting three factors as you implement our recommendations. In selecting titles and designing our teaching ideas, we have tried to address these issues. We examine them explicitly in the following paragraphs to enhance your command of literature-based teaching so that you can more effectively utilize this approach on your own.

Finding Quality Picture Books and Storybooks

Addressing this factor will not guarantee that your literature-based efforts will prove successful, but ignoring it will almost certainly doom them to failure. Selecting quality fiction is crucial for several reasons. First, good books avoid misinformation and stereotyping. They are thoroughly researched and accurately depict diversity of age, gender, physical ability, and ethnicity. Second, these works probe important topics and values-laden issues. For example, *Amazing Grace* confronts prejudice in terms that young children should understand; *The Wednesday Surprise* treats a grandmother's illiteracy in a direct, yet sensitive way. Third, quality books offer realistic situations and meaningful opportunities in which children can acquire and apply the Head, Hand, and Heart of appreciative citizenship.

How can you distinguish quality fiction from less accomplished prose? Notable books, first of all, are written in an artful, vivid style, with imagery that captures the imagination and language that flows from page to page. These books are accessible to children. Young readers relate to their themes, settings, situations, and characters. Additionally, vivid illustrations often enliven good books and reinforce their messages. Finally, authors are keen observers of the human condition. They notice behaviors and hear dialects that most people would miss. These artists convey their insights through rich, accurate descriptions that children—and adults, for that matter—find meaningful.

Most educators know a quality book when they see one. Still, identifying a title that fits just right with a particular purpose and classroom situation may not be easy. As a productive rule of thumb, begin book searches with your school or public librarians, who can trim hours from story-hunting efforts. They can point you toward Newbery and Caldecott lists. (A quick hint: Check the entire list as children often find honor books more accessible than medalists.) They can also acquaint you with state book award winners and such potential gold mines as Children's Choices, *Booklist* magazine, the National Council for the Social Studies list of "Notable Children's Trade Books in the Field of Social Studies," and recent publications specializing in diversity-related titles. Although we heartily recommend that you visit your friendly librarian first, many resources that can help you find appropriate story selections are listed in the bibliography that begins on page 123.

Sharing the Story with Children

Finding a quality book is only the first step. Somehow, children must then experience the story and construct meaning from its text and visuals. Getting young readers into a story seems an easy enough proposition: In a large group setting, assign a chapter or passage, then send each child off to read silently. After an allotted time, return students to a whole-class setting and talk over the book.

Ah, we wish life were so simple! Though this traditional approach may seem appealing, the diverse experiential and ability levels of today's primary students render it problematic. No matter how gripping the tale, it seems very unlikely that every child will possess the skills or motivation or both to finish a reading assignment. Additionally, even if everyone could comprehend the story, current budget cutbacks might render it impossible to provide 25 to 30 copies of a book.

In any event, reading the story aloud is a more efficient and more productive way to initiate literature-based instruction than individual, silent reading. Children can experience a picture book in one sitting. A storybook can be enjoyed over time as a read-aloud selection, then pressed into service as a resource for citizenship teaching (a clear case of curriculum integration if we ever saw one!). We do not claim expertise as storytellers and hesitate to coach you in the fine art of oral reading, beyond suggesting that you discover some way to transform a sharing session into a special event (e.g., dim the lights while reading; collect "tickets" as children enter the read-aloud area). Instead, we will refer you to a higher authority for more guidance—Jim Trelease's *The New Read-Aloud Handbook* (see the resources bibliography that begins on page 123). Incidentally, Trelease capsules his message in audiotapes that make wonderful listening on long car trips or daily commutes.

Besides reading silently and aloud, consider adopting one or more of these creative alternatives for sharing a story:

Form reading teams. A book for each student may not be practical, but you might track down copies for five or six small groups. Mix high- and low-ability readers and encourage them to help each other with difficult passages. Or children can read aloud to each other in round-robin fashion. Let teams regularly share their progress with the entire class.

Tape-record selected chapters. Ask a parent or, better yet, an older student to record passages on audiotape or videotape. Make these recordings available in learning centers or play them during quiet times.

Prepare story guides or summaries or both. Adult and older student volunteers can draft these reading aids.

Dramatize important incidents from the story. Cast a troupe of classroom art players to read a key passage and then role-play it live or on videotape.

Display passages from a picture book on an opaque projector. The class can read silently as you introduce a related lesson.

Deciding What to Teach and How to Teach It

A work of children's fiction can treat a diversity theme or topic and introduce related activities. However, for all its worth as a resource, a picture book or storybook will not provide learning experiences that are ready to implement. The creative teacher must take the initiative, recognizing teaching possibilities, developing them into lessons, and conducting these experiences in a classroom setting. At the same time, you need not resemble the marshal in a Western movie, facing these planning tasks all alone.

As you consider what content a book might teach, it is unnecessary to approach your decision as territory where no one has gone before. Typically, you might assume that children's stories reveal information about diversity-related topics and explore familiar, yet valuable themes. For example, these works frequently provide rich detail that furthers understanding of key concepts like prejudice, interdependence, aging, handicaps, and friendship. They introduce opportunities to develop important skills like social participation, communication, and reflective thinking. Books often convey the feel for an unfamiliar lifestyle or mindset that students might not otherwise comprehend. Stories reflect particular points of view and often deal with social issues in an open, sensitive manner, encouraging constructive dialogue about these problems.

Similarly, formulating literature-based activities is clearly the teacher's responsibility but not a challenge that must be tackled alone. After deciding what is worth teaching, you must determine how to teach it, structuring that content into a meaningful learning experience. Fortunately, a lesson format that has been classroom tested can provide a workable structure for literature-based citizenship teaching.

Cynthia Szymanski Sunal and Mary Haas (1993, 27-31) indicate that *The Learning Cycle* allows young children to construct new meaning or revamp existing knowledge. The Cycle helps them build connections between the new and the already known and apply these understandings to less familiar situations. The impetus for classroom activity rests with the students. Children not only make meanings but affirm these understandings by relating them to different contexts. They also gain insights about the thought processes that generated this knowledge and confidence in their abilities as learners. In short, children have opportunities to think, feel, and then take action as a Learning Cycle progresses.

The Cycle unfolds in three phases. During the Exploration Phase, primary students poke into an intriguing idea, personality, or event with minimal teacher guidance. They confront old ways of thinking as they raise questions, investigate an unfamiliar topic or skill, and express their discoveries to classmates. In the Invention Phase, the teacher intervenes more directly, assisting students as they develop and confirm what has been learned. Students continue to inquire but proceed in a more structured manner, involving various forms of sensory input like teacher explanations, media, text readings, trade books, and computer programs. Finally, the Expansion Phase allows young citizens to stabilize new understandings through meaningful repetition in varied situations. Students extend their grasp of a new concept or competency as they utilize it in other contexts.

The Learning Cycle offers an effective and creative structure for using children's fiction to promote appreciative citizenship. For example, a teacher might read a description of a desert locale and the traditions and customs of the people living there. Working in pairs, children can record their impressions of the setting in a detailed illustration. After children share their drawings, the teacher helps them identify essential attributes of the culture and brainstorm the ways in which geography shaped this way of life. Finally, children might illustrate lifestyles in their own community, then compare and contrast these observations with the desert way of living. The activity might conclude with a second read-and-discuss session in which children examine a story set in a forest environment.

Incorporating Learning Experiences into the Primary Curriculum

As you deal with these three factors, you must make a parallel decision that might be the trickiest issue to resolve. Where do literature-based lessons fit into your overall strategy for promoting appreciative citizenship in the primary grades? How can these experiences be utilized so they will have the most impact?

Questions about lesson placement are best answered by the teacher. Involvement with a particular set of student needs and classroom circumstances enables you to decide whether a lesson should introduce, develop, or culminate a unit of study. Although firm guidelines seem impossible to state, we can make a few suggestions about the ways in which you might integrate literature-based lessons into a citizenship program.

Literature-based learning experiences might supplement and enrich more traditional social studies lessons. For example, consider following an oral presentation with a hands-on activity suggested by a story encountered previously. Or you might read a storybook in tandem with a regular social studies unit. Share the book during story time, then draw activities from it as children proceed through the unit. Additionally, after teaching a social studies unit, you could generate a series of lessons from a related storybook as a follow-up mini-unit. Finally, you can insert a work of fiction as a teaching resource within a regular unit. Do not read the entire story; rather, insert excerpts from the book with accompanying activities as the unit progresses.

Go Forth and Teach!

Now we have tied those loose ends, and our work is complete. Our epilogue comes not as an afterthought but to support primary educators who might expand their use of literature-based teaching beyond our recommended books and activities. We encourage you to try literature-based instruction across the primary curriculum. We hope that our work broadens and deepens your students' appreciation for all citizens, regardless of their age, gender, physical ability, or ethnic background. If these learning experiences have promoted children's abilities to think, feel, and take social action, then our hopes and dreams for this book will have been realized.

References

Coles, Robert. *The Call of Stories: Teaching and the Moral Imagination.* Boston: Houghton Mifflin, 1989.

Egan, Kieran. *Teaching as Storytelling: An Alternative Approach to Teaching and Curriculum in the Elementary School.* Chicago: University of Chicago Press, 1986.

Funk & Wagnalls Standard Dictionary. New York: New American Library, 1983.

Martorella, Peter. *Elementary Social Studies: Developing Reflective, Competent, and Concerned Citizens.* Boston: Little, Brown, 1985.

Sunal, C. S., and M. E. Haas. *Social Studies and the Elementary Middle School Student.* Orlando, FL: Harcourt Brace Jovanovich, 1993.

A Bibliography of Resources

Finding Quality Picture Books and Storybooks

These resources can assist teachers in selecting quality children's literature that promotes the understandings, skills, and dispositions for appreciating age, gender, ability, and ethnic differences.

The African-American Experience: An HBJ Resource Guide for the Multicultural Classroom. Orlando, FL: Harcourt Brace Jovanovich, 1993.

Association for Library Service to Children. *The Newbery & Caldecott Awards: A Complete Listing of Medal and Honor Books.* Chicago: American Library Association, 1992. This regularly updated booklet lists the winners and runners-up for these prestigious ALA-sponsored awards. Indexed by author and title.

Carlin, Margaret, Jeannine Laughlin, and Richard Saniga. *Understanding Abilities, Disabilities, and Capabilities: A Guide to Children's Literature.* Englewood, CO: Libraries Unlimited, 1991. Recommended titles as well as helpful suggestions for teaching about the limitations and strengths of disabled people.

Children's Books: Awards and Prizes. New York: Children's Book Council, 1992. This publication describes state Children's Choice awards, including the Garden State Children's Book Award (NJ), Pacific Northwest Library Association Young Reader's Choice Award (AK, Alberta, WA, OR, MT, ID, and BC), Mark Twain Award (MO), Young Hoosier Award (IN), Golden Sower Award (NE), Young Reader Medal (CA), and Young Readers' Award (AZ).

"Children's Special Lists and Features." *Booklist* (August 1992). A compendium of lists that have appeared in earlier issues of *Booklist*. Includes many bibliographies that might illuminate diversity-related themes (e.g., immigration, intergenerational relationships, Spanish-language publications, small-press titles).

Eiss, Harry E. *Literature for Young People on War and Peace: An Annotated Bibliography.* Westport, CN: Greenwood Press, 1989. Trade books that explore conflict resolution.

"Ethnic Groups in Children's Books." *Booklist.* This ALA-sponsored journal periodically provides bibliographies of literature featuring themes, settings, and characters related to particular ethnic groups.

Friedberg, Joan. *Portraying Persons with Disabilities: An Annotated Bibliography of Non-Fiction for Children and Teenagers*, 2d ed. New Providence, NJ: Bowker, 1992. This reference provides a current, comprehensive listing of books dealing with physical, mental, and emotional handicaps.

123

Galda, Lee, and Susan Cox. "Books for Cross-Cultural Understanding." *The Reading Teacher* (April 1991): 580-586. Extensive bibliographic essay describing books that promote cross-cultural understanding; grouped by geographic region or cultural group.

International Reading Association. "Children's Choices." A preference list published every October in *The Reading Teacher*. For single copies of this list, write IRA; ATTN: Children's Choices; P. O. Box 8139; Newark, DE 19714.

Jenkins, Esther C. *Literature for Children About Asians and Asian-Americans.* Westport, CN: Greenwood Press, 1987. Thorough, if a bit dated, list of books with Asian and Asian-American themes.

Kalisa, Beryl Graham. "Africa in Picture Books: Portrait or Preconception." *School Library Journal* (February 1990): 36-37. Bibliographic essay that critically examines recent picture books with African themes.

Lee, Lauren K., ed. *Elementary School Library Collection: A Guide to Books and Other Media.* Williamsport, PA: Brodart, 1992. Indexed listing of available print and nonprint materials appropriate for grades pre-K to six.

Lettow, Lucille, and Jeanne Harmes. "Popular Reading—Historical Fiction." *Booklist* (March 1, 1988): 1189. Bibliography of historical fiction for children has been compiled under ALA-sponsorship and includes books with American and world history themes.

Lewis, Valerie, and Monica Holmes. "Best Books for Teaching with Themes." *Instructor* (August 1991): 36-39. Representative of a growing number of features on literature-based teaching that *Instructor* has recently published.

Miller-Lachmann, L. *Our Family, Our Friends, Our World: An Annotated Guide to Significant Multicultural Books for Children and Teenagers.* New Providence, NJ: Bowker, 1992. Provides annotated bibliographies of related literature for studying about cultures within our society and around the world.

National Council for the Social Studies. "Notable Children's Trade Books in the Field of Social Studies." Published annually in the April/May issue of *Social Education.* A tremendously useful resource prepared by NCSS in collaboration with the Children's Book Council.

Recommended Books and Historical Literature for the History-Social Science Framework for the California Public Schools, Kindergarten Through Grade Twelve. Sacramento, CA: California State Department of Education, 1988. Annotated list of literature that supplements California's state social studies curriculum.

Robertson, Debra. *Portraying Persons with Disabilities: An Annotated Bibliography of Fiction for Children and Teenagers*, 3d ed. New Providence, NJ: Bowker, 1992.

Rollock, Barbara. *Black Authors and Illustrators of Children's Books: A Biographical Dictionary*, 2d edition. New York: Garland, 1992. Up-to-date background information about black authors and their work.

Schon, Isabel. *A Hispanic Heritage, Series IV: A Guide to Juvenile Books About Hispanic People and Cultures.* Metuchen, NJ: Scarecrow Press, 1991. A K-12 bibliography that encompasses literature from most of the world's Hispanic countries and peoples.

Schreiber, Joan. *Using Children's Books in Social Studies, Early Childhood Through Primary Grades.* NCSS Bulletin 71. Washington, DC: National Council for the Social Studies, 1984. Pioneering essay that identifies social studies-related titles for young children.

Slapin, Beverly, and Doris Seale. *Through Indian Eyes: The Native American Experience in Books for Children.* Philadelphia: New Society, 1992. Critical reviews of literature about Native Americans from an Indian perspective.

"The USA Through Children's Books." *Booklist* (May 1, 1988): 1532 and (May 1, 1990): 1713. The bibliographies feature our nation's history, geography, and cultures.

VanMeter, Vandelia. *American History for Children and Young Adults: An Annotated Bibliographic Index.* Englewood, CO: Libraries Unlimited, 1990. An annotated listing of trade books that personalize and familiarize the past.

————. *World History for Children and Young Adults: An Annotated Bibliographic Index.* Englewood, CO: Libraries Unlimited, 1992. Includes fiction and nonfiction selections.

Williams, Helen E. *Books by African-American Authors and Illustrators for Children and Young Adults.* Chicago: American Library Association, 1991. Useful tool providing biographical information and summaries of quality literature.

Wilms, Denise, ed. *A Guide to Non-Sexist Children's Books,* Volume II (1976-1985). Chicago: Academy, 1987. Literature featuring nonsexist themes and language.

Sharing the Story with Children

These resources offer creative storytelling and read-aloud ideas that engage children and help them make meaning from text. They also recommend stories, media, and books that have strong share-aloud potential.

Bauer, Caroline Feller. *Handbook for Storytellers.* Chicago: American Library Association, 1977. Although Bauer focuses on the art of storytelling, folktales, and oral history, she includes a helpful section on reading books aloud to groups of children.

Hunt, Mary Alice. *A Multimedia Approach to Children's Literature.* 3d ed. Chicago: American Library Association, 1983. Hunt catalogs audiovisual materials (e.g., filmstrips, audiotapes, kits) that present selected works of children's literature in alternative ways.

Ralston, Marion V. *An Exchange of Gifts: A Storyteller's Handbook.* Portsmouth, NH: Heinemann, 1993.

Trelease, Jim. *The New Read-Aloud Handbook.* 2d rev. ed. New York: Penguin, 1989. A classic from a leader in the read-aloud movement. Also available on audiotape.

Deciding What to Teach and How to Teach It

These articles and activity guides provide practical tips for integrated learning experiences that might boost students' understanding of and respect for diversity. As literature-based instruction has assumed greater visibility in recent years, advocates have produced increasing quantities of high-quality teaching resources.

Anderson, Nancy. "Using Children's Literature to Teach Black American History." *The Social Studies* (March/April 1977): 88-89.

Austin, Mary, and Esther Jenkins. *Promoting World Understanding Through Literature, K-8.* Littleton, CO: Libraries Unlimited, 1983.

Barr, Ian, and Margit McGuire. "Social Studies and Effective Stories." *Social Studies and the Young Learner* (January/February 1993): 6-8.

Billig, Edith. "Children's Literature as a Springboard to the Content Areas." *The Reading Teacher* (May 1977): 855-859.

Branson, Margaret S. *Tradebooks and the Social Studies: A Special Relationship.* Mini-Seminars on Using Books Creatively. New York: Children's Book Council, 1979. Audiotape.

Brozo, William, and Carl Tomlinson. "Literature: The Key to Lively Content Courses." *The Reading Teacher* (December 1986): 288-293.

Caduto, Michael, and Joseph Bruchac. *Keepers of the Earth: Native American Stories and Environmental Activities for Children.* Golden, CO: Fulcrum, 1989.

———. *Keepers of the Animals: Native American Stories and Wildlife Activities for Children.* Golden, CO: Fulcrum, 1991.

Coles, Robert. *The Call of Stories: Teaching and the Moral Imagination.* Boston: Houghton Mifflin, 1989.

Danielson, Kathy Everts. "Helping History Come Alive with Literature." *The Social Studies* (March/April 1989): 65-68.

Davis, John, and Jesse Palmer. "A Strategy for Using Children's Literature to Extend the Social Studies Curriculum." *The Social Studies* (May/June 1992): 125-128.

Egan, Kieran. *Teaching as Storytelling: An Alternative Approach to Teaching and Curriculum in the Elementary School.* Chicago: University of Chicago Press, 1986.

Fassler, Joan, and Marjorie Graham Janis. "Books, Children, and Peace." *Social Education* (September 1985): 493-497.

Fredericks, Anthony. *Social Studies Through Children's Literature: An Integrated Approach.* Englewood, CO: Libraries Unlimited, 1991.

Fuhler, Carol J. "Add Spark and Sizzle to Middle School Social Studies." *The Social Studies* (November/December 1991): 234-237.

Gallagher, Arlene. "Children's Literature and the Ethics Dimension." *Social Studies and the Young Learner* (September/October 1988): 25-27.

Hansen, Miriam, and K. C. Schmidt. "Promoting Global Awareness Through Trade Books." *The Middle School Journal* (September 1989): 34-37.

Hennings, Dorothy. "Reading Picture Storybooks in the Social Studies." *The Reading Teacher* (December 1982): 284-289.

"Integrating Language Arts and Social Studies." *Social Education* (December 1992). Theme issue exploring possibilities for literature, language expression, and social studies.

Jorgensen-Esmaili, K. "Making the Reading, Writing, Social Studies Connection." *Social Studies and the Young Learner* (March/April 1990): 20-22.

Keach, Everett, Jr. "Social Studies Instruction Through Children's Literature." *The Elementary School Journal* (November 1974): 98-102.

Lamme, Linda, Suzanne Krogh, and K. Yachmetz. *Literature-Based Moral Education: Children's Books and Activities for Teaching Values, Responsibility, and Good Judgment in the Elementary School.* Phoenix: Oryx Press, 1992.

Laughlin, Mildred K., and Patricia P. Kardaleff. *Literature-Based Social Studies: Children's Books and Activities to Enrich the K-5 Curriculum.* Phoenix: Oryx Press, 1991.

Levstik, Linda S. "A Child's Approach to History." *The Social Studies* (November/December 1983): 232-236.

Levstik, Linda S., and Evelyn Freeman. "Recreating the Past: Historical Fiction in the Social Studies Curriculum." *The Elementary School Journal* (March 1988): 329-337.

McElmeel, Sharron L. *Adventures with Social Studies (Through Literature).* Englewood, CO: Libraries Unlimited, 1991. Activities for MS/JHS.

McGowan, Tom, and Barbara Guzzetti. "Promoting Social Studies Understanding Through Literature-Based Instruction." *The Social Studies* (January/February 1991): 16-21.

McGowan, Tom, and Meredith McGowan. *Children, Literature, and Social Studies: Activities for the Intermediate Grades.* Indianapolis, IN: Special Literature Press, 1986.

McGowan, Tom, and Meredith McGowan. *Integrating the Primary Curriculum: Social Studies and Children's Literature.* Indianapolis, IN: Special Literature Press, 1988.

McGowan, Tom, and Meredith McGowan. *Telling America's Story: Teaching American History Through Children's Literature.* Hilton Head Island, SC: Child Graphics Press, 1989.

Rasinski, Timothy V., and Nancy D. Padak. "Multicultural Learning Through Children's Literature." *Language Arts* (October 1990): 576-580.

Rasinski, Timothy V., and Cindy S. Gillespie. *Sensitive Issues: An Annotated Guide to Children's Literature, K-6.* Phoenix: Oryx Press, 1992.

Roberts, Patricia L. *A Green Dinosaur Day: A Guide for Developing Thematic Units in Literature-Based Instruction, K-6.* Boston: Allyn and Bacon, 1993.

Sanacore, J. "Creating the Lifetime Reading Habit in Social Studies." *Journal of Reading* (March 1990): 414-418.

Smith, John, and Dorothy Dobson. "Teaching with Historical Novels: A Four-Step Approach." *Social Studies and the Young Learner* (January/February 1993): 19-22.

Walter, Virginia A. *War and Peace: Literature for Children and Young Adults.* Phoenix: Oryx Press, 1993.

Wheeler, Ann. "Individualizing Instruction in Social Studies Through the Use of Children's Literature." *The Social Studies* (April 1971): 166-171.

Zarrillo, James. "History and Library Books." *Social Studies and the Young Learner* (November/December 1989): 17-19.

Index

About the Authors

Meredith McGowan grew up in Nebraska and graduated from Wayne State College in 1970. She earned a master of science in educational media administration from the University of Nebraska-Omaha in 1982 and a masters in library science from Indiana University-Bloomington in 1988. Her career has included positions as a media specialist in several Nebraska schools, as a public librarian in Indiana, and as a faculty associate in the Reading and Library Science department, College of Education, Arizona State University. She has long been interested in connecting children's literature with the school curriculum, especially social studies.

Tom McGowan grew up in Massachusetts and Delaware and graduated from Boston University in 1970. After serving two years in the Army, he obtained a master of arts in history from the University of Nebraska-Lincoln in 1974 and earned his Ph.D. in education in 1983. He taught elementary-school children for five years, and spent five years teaching at Indiana State University, Terre Haute. Since 1988, he has taught social studies courses at Arizona State University, Tempe, encouraging his students to become competent and creative social educators.

Pat Wheeler has experienced children and teachers from several sides of the desk. Educated at Southern Illinois University, Carbondale, she received her bachelors in 1968, her master of science in 1974, and her Ph.D. in 1987. She started her career teaching first graders how to read, then spent 12 years as a school library-media specialist for elementary and middle schools, and now teaches college students who want to become teachers. She likes to help teachers use student-centered reading and language arts as tools for integrating all curriculum areas. She also consults with teachers who are examining their own teaching. Pat is currently an Associate Professor in the Department of Elementary/Early Childhood Education at Indiana State University, Terre Haute, where she works with all levels of preservice and inservice teachers.

135